Dedication

Dedicated to the millions of private collectors, who, over the centuries, have filled our museums and deciphered our history, all for the love of knowledge.

Acknowledgments

Special thanks to the following
for providing the spectacular color
photography that made this book possible:

Coins

Heritage Numismatic Auctions, Inc.
3500 Maple Ave., 17th Floor
Dallas, TX 75219-3941
214-528-3500
800-US COINS (872-6467)
Bid@HeritageCoins.com
View full-color images at coins.ha.com

Paper Money

Chester L. Krause

Warman's® Identification and Price Guides

Warman's® American & European Art Pottery
Warman's® Antiques & Collectibles Annual
    Price Guide
Warman's® Carnival Glass
Warman's® Children's Books
Warman's® Civil War Collectibles
Warman's® Civil War Weapons
Warman's® Coca-Cola® Collectibles
Warman's® Coins and Paper Money
Warman's® Cookie Jars
Warman's® Costume Jewelry Figurals
Warman's® Depression Glass
Warman's® Dolls: Antique to Modern
Warman's® Duck Decoys
Warman's® English & Continental Pottery & Porcelain
Warman's® Fenton Glass
Warman's® Fiesta
Warman's® Flea Market Price Guide
Warman's® Gas Station Collectibles
Warman's® Hull Pottery
Warman's® Jewelry
Warman's® John Deere Collectibles
Warman's® Little Golden Books®
Warman's® Majolica
Warman's® McCoy Pottery
Warman's® Modernism Furniture and Accessories
Warman's® North American Indian Artifacts
Warman's® Political Collectibles
Warman's® Red Wing Pottery
Warman's® Rookwood Pottery
Warman's® Roseville Pottery
Warman's® Sporting Collectibles
Warman's® Sterling Silver Flatware
Warman's® Vietnam War Collectibles
Warman's® Vintage Jewelry
Warman's® Vintage Quilts
Warman's® Weller Pottery
Warman's® World War II Collectilbes

Warman's® Companions

Carnival Glass Warman's® Companion
Collectible Dolls Warman's® Companion
Collectible Fishing Lures Warman's® Companion
Depression Glass Warman's® Companion
Fenton Glass Warman's® Companion
Fiesta Warman's® Companion
Hallmark Keepsake Ornaments
    Warman's® Companion
Hot Wheels Warman's® Companion
McCoy Pottery Warman's® Companion
PEZ® Warman's® Companion
Roseville Pottery Warman's® Companion
Watches Warman's® Companion
World Coins & Currency Warman's®
Companion

Warman's® Field Guides

Warman's® Action Figures Field Guide
Warman's® Antique Jewelry Field Guide
Warman's® Barbie Doll Field Guide
Warman's® Bean Plush Field Guide
Warman's® Bottles Field Guide
Warman's® Buttons Field Guide
Warman's® Coca-Cola® Field Guide
Warman's® Depression Glass Field Guide
Warman's® Disney Collectibles Field Guide
Warman's® Dolls Field Guide
Warman's® Farm Toys Field Guide
Warman's® Field Guide to Precious Moments®
Warman's® Fishing Lures Field Guide
Warman's® G.I. Joe Field Guide
Warman's® Hot Wheels Field Guide
Warman's® Kitschy Kitchen Collectibles Field
    Guide
Warman's® Lionel Train Field Guide 1945-1969
Warman's® Lunch Boxes Field Guide
Warman's® Matchbox Field Guide
Warman's® Pepsi Field Guide
Warman's® Star Wars Field Guide
Warman's® Tools Field Guide
Warman's® Transformers Field Guide
Warman's® U.S. Coins & Currency Field Guide
Warman'® U.S. Stamps Field Guide
Warman's® Vintage Guitars Field Guide
Warman's® Watches Field Guide
Warman's® Zippo Lighters Field Guide

Contents

CONTENTS

Introduction

This book is not intended to be a comprehensive resource about coins and paper money. In fact, a full library is necessary to answer every question regarding this subject. Rather, it is intended to fill a much needed niche—a very basic introduction in which a reader can get a quick overview of the hobby, and get a general feel for the background, characteristics and values of each of the common categories presented.

Because this book is only an introduction to the subject, only brief information is given on early coins and paper money, and photos and listings focus on items from the early 1800s and later, which are the items most likely to be encountered today.

Values

Coin and currency prices can be as volatile as the stock market. While some coins and bills remain stable for years, others skyrocket during a period of popularity and then plummet when they fall out of fashion. The listings presented here simply give an idea of the normal retail value at the time of writing. Because the law of supply and demand ultimately rules, the final decision about the value of a coin lies with the buyer and seller.

Dealers are in business to make a living. This means they must pay less than the retail cost listed in this book when they are buying. Depending on the value and demand, a dealer will pay between 10 and 90 percent of the retail value of coins or currency listed in this reference.

Finally, the grades chosen to represent average prices are those most likely found in the market or the ones most likely to be sought by the average collector.

Sizes

Coins and paper money are not shown to scale in this book. Most coins have been enlarged to show more detail, and all paper money has been reduced to fit the pages. Thus, do not rely on the size of the photos for identification, but rather the information stamped or printed on the coins or bills, and the captions and listings accompanying them.

State of the Market

In marked contrast to the general economy, the coin market over the past year has been to quite strong, continuing a trend established over the previous three years. Both U.S. and world coin dealers are reporting demand as being anywhere from healthy to robust. This does not however mean that the present market is performing according to traditional expectations.

The most glaring anomaly is the growing "disconnect" between the "spot price" and the gold and silver markets for actual physical delivery. Spot price is the value typically quoted by the media and technically reflects the value of a contract for a fixed number of ounces tradable on the commodity exchange.

No physical object such as a coin or ingot is actually handed from a seller to a buyer. In a normal market the price a dealer would pay for an actual bullion coin, an ounce of gold for example, is based on the spot price plus or minus a minimal commission of two or three percent. A dealer's selling price would be perhaps three to six percent over that.

At present, the United States Mint is not able to ship enough bullion coins to meet demand—when it ships at all. It has recently refused to release Silver Eagles, but demand for them is unabated. As a result, premiums are being forced by the market to unprecedented levels. Dealers are willing to pay as much as 10 percent over spot price for standard items such as U.S. Gold Eagles and Canadian Maple leafs, and are retailing them for well over that. Some are trading as much as $100 per ounce premium when the customer will not wait. It seems that the spot price has not been reflecting the real market for actual gold and silver. Hence, these nominal prices are not able to induce sellers to release bullion onto the market. Will this dichotomy between paper and physical bullion cease, or will there soon be two distinct and fully acknowledged markets? We shall see.

This situation has had its affect on more common numismatic coins too, not just bullion items. Many coins with a collector premium, but a small one, have been behaving similarly. These include antique $20 gold pieces and old British gold sovereigns. Possibly fueled by economic uncertainty, even pure hobbyist coins have been subject to constant demand. Perhaps those of us with steady jobs see coin collecting as a less frivolous hobby than other pursuits. In a pinch, there will always be something left to sell if one is a coin collector, even if the larger dealer profit margins on hobbyist coins are enough to take such pieces out of the category of pure investment.

The declining U.S. dollar has been forcing the prices of better world coins upwards. American dealers are constantly having to pay more and more for popular coins such as those of Britain, Italy, and Germany, and the early issues of the Roman Empire. Home country demand for Russia and Poland in particular have been intense. The new values for these series have steamrolled over everybody's old pricing preconceptions.

Overall, veteran dealers are bewildered by the present state of the market. Making a profit is easy, but there is a whole new set of rules for what is hot, what is out there to buy, and what premiums are appropriate to pull in new material and make it sell again. Remember the Chinese curse: May you live in interesting times.

Coin Introduction

Evolution of U.S. Coins

An average American living in the 13 Colonies during the 18th century would not have found many English silver or gold coins in his pocket. It was British policy to restrict the export of precious metals to the Colonies. As a result, nothing but copper was struck for the Colonies, and even that was rarely minted.

Silver coins were so scarce in the Colonies that Colonial Americans used any other foreign silver or gold coin that could be pressed into service. Besides Spanish coins, French, Portuguese, and occasionally German silver and gold were readily accepted when they turned up.

French Colonies 1762A Sou Marque

Some of the Colonial governors also issued paper money valued in terms of discounted British currency, or in Spanish milled dollars. After the Declaration of Independence, many of the same forms of currency continued. Spanish Colonial silver and gold were as popular as ever. All the new states issued their own paper money.

Under the Articles of Confederation, the first United States Constitution, each state was essentially a fully sovereign country, some of them issued official state-sanctioned coinage.

When the Constitution took effect in 1789, it put an end to all state-issued coinage. In view of the new, stronger federal union, many people began to take the idea of a single national coinage more seriously. Others argued that it was not the place of government to get involved in such things. With the personal

1787 Continental Congress Fugio Cent

influence of George Washington himself behind them, the proponents of the new United States Mint persevered, and construction began in 1792.

For both administrative and technical reasons, the Mint got off to a slow start, but before the end of the year, silver five-cent pieces struck from the first president's tableware were circulating around Philadelphia. The new coinage was based on a decimal system dividing a dollar into 100 cents. The idea of the dollar as the standard unit was inspired by the Spanish piece of eight, then common in the Colonies.

Suffering under a severe shortage of both bullion and labor, as well as annual epidemics of yellow fever, the early Mint never succeeded in placing substantial coinage in circulation on a national level. Broad circulation was also prevented by the rapid withdrawal and melting of much of the gold and silver coinage by speculators, because American coins had too high a precious metal content relative to their value. The endeavor became so futile that the striking of many denominations was frequently suspended. It wasn't until the 1830s that the weights of the coins were adjusted to prevent their export.

During the Mint's first four decades, every die was engraved by hand, so no two looked alike. Also, the coins were struck by hand on a screw press one at a time. Finally, in 1836, the Industrial Revolution came to the U.S. Mint. Steam-powered striking equipment was imported from England. Almost overnight American coins became more neat and uniform. The old lettered edges were replaced by modern reeding, the hundreds of parallel lines found on coins today.

Also, the quantities that could be produced in the same amount of time increased drastically. This technological improvement roughly coincided with the needed reduction in the coins' bullion content and with a facelift for all silver denominations. Thus, during the mid-1830s, the nation's coinage was utterly transformed.

1873 Silver Three-Cent Piece

The silver three-cent piece and three new gold denominations, $3 (1854) and $1 and $20 (1849) were introduced, partially because of the California gold rush.

1860S Gold Three-Dollar Piece

But the big event of the mid-century was the coinage law of 1857. This one act eliminated the half-cent, reduced the size of the one-cent piece from bigger than a quarter to the diameter used today and, most importantly, caused foreign silver and gold to cease to be legal tender in the United States. The Mint was finally able to produce enough to provide a true national coinage.

Civil War coin shortages not only resulted in many private tokens, but also inspired the two-cent and nickel three-cent pieces, and later possibly the five-cent nickel. It also saw the debut of the motto "In God We Trust" on the coinage. During the late 1860s and 1870s the nation was in the economic doldrums. Mintages were low for many denominations, particularly the silver dollar. Hence, many coins are scarce today.

1885 Nickel Three-Cent Piece

From the late 1870s onward, coinage was plentiful for half a century—sometimes too plentiful. A dominant political influence was the "Free Silver Movement," which didn't mean people wanted to be given free silver, but that they wanted unlimited quantities to be converted into coin to use up the excess that was being mined. They also intended that this increase the money supply, thereby causing inflation to erode debts.

1879O Morgan Dollar

From 1873 to 1918, and later, several laws were passed to force the government to buy silver and strike an abundance of silver dollars. Unpopular in the more developed parts of the country, the dollar coins frequently sat in government or bank vaults for decades. Minor silver also became more common during this era.

Early in the 20th century, Theodore Roosevelt led the nation to a new level of intellectual consciousness, touching on ideas as diverse as national parks

1942 Walking Liberty Half Dollar

and the artistic merits of the nation's coinage. For the latter, he sought the aid of the greatest sculptors of the day, deliberately looking outside the Mint staff for talent. Most of the new coin designs reflect neo-classical artistic trends also prevalent in Europe. The beautiful designs include the Mercury dime, the Walking Liberty half, and the St. Gaudens double eagle, as well as the less classically inspired Buffalo nickel.

1943S Zinc-Coated Steel Lincoln Cent

A commemorative coin program was also getting underway, providing an outlet for artists of various tastes. Most never saw circulation, being sold at a premium to collectors. By 1936, this had gotten so far out of hand that in that one year alone, 22 different half dollars were struck!

The need for strategic metals for armaments during World War II was the cause for interesting, if not pleasant, aberrations in the cent and nickel. The striking of these in steel and a silver-manganese alloy respectively was a response to these shortages.

1943P Jefferson Nickel

Idealistic images of Liberty were gradually replaced during the 1930s and 1940s with those of statesmen, and artists were determined by contests rather than by selection.

2006S Nevada State Quarter

An increase in the price of silver in 1964 prompted massive hoarding of silver coins as their content approached their face value. As a result, silver was partially or completely removed from coinage in favor of clad coinage, which can be readily distinguished by the copper core visible on the edge. Almost 30 years later the cent was also debased, with bronze alloy being replaced by one of zinc simply plated with bronze.

Today, the nation's coinage is characterized by a new flood of commemoratives struck for both significant and insignificant reasons, most completely unknown to the American people. Traditionally sold at a high premium by the Mint, commemoratives circulated at face value in 1999 for the first time since the Bicentennial.

The five 1999 state quarters were the first issues in a 10-year series commemorating each state. The state quarter series was well received by the public and has been credited with creating significant growth in the popularity of coin collecting in the U.S.

Coin Mints and Mintmarks

The first U.S. Mint was constructed in Philadelphia in 1792. Over the centuries, the continuously growing facility has had several different homes in that city. Officially, all other mints are branch mints, but this does not mean that the largest quantities of each coin are always struck in Philadelphia.

The first branch mints were opened to strike coins from new gold being mined from deposits found in the South. These mints in Charlotte, N.C., and Dahlonega, Ga., were opened in 1838 and closed at the start of the Civil War in 1861. They never struck in any metal but gold, usually in small quantities. Also opened for the same duration, but of far greater importance, was the New Orleans Mint. This became the second largest mint, striking vast numbers of coins in both gold and silver.

The San Francisco Mint was opened in 1854 in response to the California Gold Rush. Today, it strikes most of the proof issues. In 1870, the silver mining boom in Nevada caused the Mint to open a branch in Carson City. It was closed in 1893, and its coins are generally scarce.

Easily rivaling Philadelphia in its present importance is the Denver Mint. Opened in 1906, it sometimes strikes more coins than the primary Mint itself.

Recently, some coins have been struck at West Point, N.Y. These are not circulation strikes, but collector issues and bullion only.

One can usually tell where a coin is struck by its mintmark, a small letter or a mark placed on the coin. In the United States, they have usually been on the reverse, but re-appeared on the obverse after they were removed from 1965 to 1967. The following are mintmarks used on United States coins:

none – Philadelphia, Pa.
P – Philadelphia
C – Charlotte, N.C.
CC – Carson City, Nev.
D – Dahlonega, Ga.
D – Denver, Colo.
O – New Orleans, La.
S – San Francisco, Calif.
W – West Point, N.Y.

Coin Grading

The value of a coin is in part determined by its "grade," or state of preservation. The most basic part of grading is determining how much a coin is worn. To describe a coin that is not present, such as in correspondence, numismatists have agreed on a series of terms to describe how much wear there is on a coin. Following are the grades from best (no wear at all) to worst (worn out):

> Uncirculated (Mint State)
> Brilliant Uncirculated
> About Uncirculated
> Extremely Fine (Extra Fine)
> Very Fine
> Fine
> Very Good
> Good
> Fair
> Poor

For every type of U.S. and Canadian coin, very specific criteria have been agreed on for each degree of wear. For U.S. coins, these criteria were developed under the auspices of the American Numismatic Association and have been published in the *Official A.N.A. Grading Standards for United States Coins,* usually called "The Gray Book." It is carried and used by virtually every coin shop. Following are some illustrations of examples of coins in each state of wear, with some of the basic requirements for that grade.

Uncirculated (Unc.) or Mint State (MS) coins, those with no wear at all, as though they had just come from the Mint, have been divided into 11 basic categories, from 60 to 70, the latter being best. The reason for this is that even with no circulation at all, the coins themselves do hit each other while stored at the Mint in large bags, leaving minute scuffs. These scuffs are called "bag marks." While these 11 points are a continuum, the ANA has not traditionally recognized intermediate grades other than the ones listed in this book, but many coin dealers do. When a legendary numismatic scholar and cataloger was asked if he could tell an MS-61 from an MS-62, he replied "No. Neither, I think, can anyone else. It is simply ammunition for those whose motivation is dishonesty and greed."

Uncirculated or Mint-State coins with absolutely no bag marks or any other problems are called MS-70, but these perfect coins do not really exist for most series. To be MS-70, a coin must be fully struck and have no unpleasant stains or discoloration.

BU (Brilliant Uncirculated) refers to a Mint State coin retaining all or most of its original luster. It may have a numeric grade of MS-60 to MS-70. In the case of higher grades, many dealers prefer to use the more precise numeric grades.

MS-67

MS-67 is the nearest thing to a perfect coin that is likely to be practically obtainable. It may have the faintest of bag marks discernible only through a magnifying glass. Copper must have luster.

MS-65

MS-65 is a grade describing an exceptional coin. It is the highest grade that can be easily obtained when conservative grading is used. It will have no significant bag marks, particularly in open areas such as the field or the cheek. Copper may have toning. Fewer than one coin in hundreds qualifies for this grade, and is one of the most popular grade of coins with investors.

MS-63

MS-63 coins are pleasant, collectible examples that exhibit enough bag marks to be noticed, but not so many as to be considered marred, with particularly few on open areas such as the field or the cheek.

MS-60

MS-60 describes those coins that were very much scuffed up at the Mint before their release. They will often have nicks and discoloration. Sometimes called "commercial uncirculated," they may actually be less pleasant to behold than a higher grade circulated coin.

AU

About Uncirculated (AU) describes coins with such slight signs of wear that some people may in fact need a mild magnifying glass to see them. A trace of luster should be visible. One should be careful not to confuse an attractive AU coin for Uncirculated.

EF

Extremely Fine (EF or XF) is the highest grade of coin that exhibits wear significant enough to be seen easily by the unaided eye. It is a coin that still exhibits extremely clear minute detail. In the case of American coins featuring the word "LIBERTY" on a headband or shield, all letters must be sharp and clear. Many coins will exhibit luster, but it is not necessary.

VF

Very Fine (VF) coins show obvious signs of wear. Nevertheless, most of the detail of the design is still clear. It is an overall pleasant coin. On American coins with "LIBERTY" on a headband or shield, all letters must be clear.

F

Fine (F) is the lowest grade most people would consider collectible. About half the design details show for most types. On U.S. coins with "LIBERTY" described above, all letters must be visible if not sharp.

VG

Very Good (VG) coins exhibit heavy wear. All outlines are clear, as is generally the rim. Some internal detail also shows, but most is worn off. At least three letters of "LIBERTY" described above must be legible, all letters on pre-1857 copper and Morgan dollars.

G

Good (G) coins are generally considered uncollectible except for novelty purposes. The design usually shows no internal detail at all. Some of the rim may also be worn out. As described above, "LIBERTY" is worn off on most coins and shows just trace elements on pre-1857 copper and Morgan dollars.

AG

About Good (AG) and Fair (FR) are grades in which only truly scarce coins are collected. Many collectors would rather do without a coin than to add it to their collections. The rim will be worn down and some outline to the design may be gone.

FR

Poor (PR) is the lowest possible grade. Many coins graded Poor will not even be identifiable. When identifiable, many will still be condemned to the melting pot. Few collectors would consider owning such a coin except in the case of the most extreme rarities.

Sometimes treated as a grade, but technically not one at all is **Proof (PF)**. Proof quality is a special way of making coins for presentation. A proof coin is usually double struck with highly polished dies on polished blanks, yielding a mirror-like finish. These days, the Mint mass-markets proof coins to collectors.

Proof

In the past, matte or sandblast proofs were popular, characterized by a non-reflective but highly detailed surface. Cameo proof is a particular kind of proof that has been struck with dies polished only in the fields, but with the details such as the portrait deliberately given a dull finish. For some coins, these cameo proofs have a premium value above regular proofs. Proofs often grade MS-65 or higher.

Other miscellaneous factors can affect the quality of a coin. The presence of all or part of the original luster usually increases a coin's value. Be careful, however, not to be fooled by a coin that has been dipped in a brightener to simulate this luster artificially.

Toning can be good or bad. If the toning a coin has acquired is dull, irregular, or splotchy, it is likely to be considered unpleasant, and many collectors may choose to avoid it even if it is a high-grade coin.

On the other hand, if the toning is mild or displays a "halo effect" around the edge of the coin, or is composed of pleasant iridescent shades, many collectors and dealers would consider paying a premium to obtain it based on its "eye appeal." Standard phrases used to emphasize a coin's eye appeal when grading include Premium Quality (PQ) and Proof Like (PL).

Also, the Mint will sometimes strike a coin on a blank that is properly prepared enough not to be considered an error, but is nevertheless in some minor way imperfect. The poor mixing of the metals in the alloy, or flaws left by trapped gas from this same process, are examples. If trivial, they may be ignored on most coins, but on more expensive or high-grade pieces, the level of concern over these flaws may increase.

Even on circulated coins, few collectors wish to have scratches or edge nicks. These will occur even more frequently on larger coins like silver dollars or on coins with reeded edges. Depending on extent, such coins may be discounted by a little or a lot.

Ideal Toning

Poor Toning

   Of course, coins with damage are worth far less than coins without. Many coins have been mounted for use in jewelry, and even when the loop or bezel has been removed, they may still show slight signs of this unfortunate experience. A few collectors consider these situations opportunities to acquire coins with high-grade detail for a fraction of the cost. It should be remembered that the same heavy discount will apply when the collector resells the coins.

Handling and Treatment of Coins

How a collector treats their coins can greatly affect how well they hold their value. Metal is more reactive and softer than most people think.

The human body contains many corrosive chemicals. In some cases, simply touching a coin can contribute to its deterioration. This is especially true of coins exhibiting mint luster or iridescent toning. Touching a bright copper surface with a sweaty thumb can easily result in the appearance of a dark thumbprint several weeks or months later.

All this being said, it is easy to understand why the first lesson of coin collecting is to **never touch a coin on its surface**. If one needs to pick up a coin with bare skin, touch only its edge. In the case of proof coins, even greater precaution must be taken. The highly reflective surfaces are so sensitive that one should avoid even breathing directly on a coin. This will create small black dots that coin collectors call "carbon spots." Also, do not leave coins where they can be directly exposed to dust, sunlight, or changes in temperature.

To Clean or Not to Clean Coins?

Many new collectors ask the question "How do I remove the toning?" While it can be done, it is not recommended. While there are rare exceptions when it is beneficial, it should generally be stated that one should **never clean a coin**. It is highly likely that more harm than good will result. Toning is actually part of the coin. It is molecularly bonded to the metal, and the only way to remove the toning is to remove part of the coin. This is the way in which most coin dips work, by means of a mild acid. Physical cleaning is even worse, as microscopic striations almost inevitably are scraped into the coin's surface even using materials as mild as a tissue!

Coin Storage

Coins can be stored in many ways. One of the most convenient is in two-inch square plastic "flips." These are transparent holders with two pockets, one to contain the coin, one to contain a cardboard ticket on which information can be recorded. It folds over on itself into a size two inches by two inches. Originally, they were made only of a PVC formula plastic. This material was particularly flexible and easy to work with, but eventually it would break down, depositing a green slime on the coins it contained.

Today both the PVC formula and a new, more inert Mylar formula are available. The Mylar type is prone to cracking, but so far has not been found to damage coins. The PVC type is still popular because it is more flexible, but it is now used only by dealers and auction houses for temporary storage. Collectors usually repackage coins purchased in such holders before placing a coin into long-term storage.

Another common coin holder is the "two-by-two." This is a pair of cardboard squares with an adhering film of relatively inert plastic on one side. The coin is sandwiched between the two layers of plastic, and the two halves are stapled together. While this does not permit the coin to be removed and touched as easily as storage in flips, it does permit the coin to be viewed on both sides without opening the holder.

It is important to be very careful when removing coins from these holders so the coin is not accidentally scratched on the exposed ends of the staples that poke out when the holder is pulled apart. These careless staple scratches have ruined tens of thousands of good coins.

Both flips and two-by-twos fit nicely into specially made boxes. They also fit into plastic pages designed to hold 20 of either holder. The pages are transparent and will fit into most loose-leaf binders. It is important to remember not to place coins loose in the pages, as they are often of PVC plastic. Moreover, some of the thumb-cuts made to help remove the coins are large enough for some coins to fall through.

Many specialized coin folders and albums are designed not only to store and exhibit a collection, but to guide collectors. Each coin in the series is individually labeled, making the holder very convenient. It is widely believed that one of the main reasons coin collecting was able to catch on with the American middle class in the 1930s is the invention of the "penny board," a one-sheet predecessor of these modern coin folders and albums.

Old folders and albums are made by different processes than present ones. Older ones contained substances in the cardboard that tone the coins, although actual corrosion is rare. Today, most manufacturers omit these materials from their albums.

The toning also occurs with the long-term use of the orange-brown two-inch coin envelopes, although it is less of a problem with those of other colors. The toning in this case is caused by sulfur in the paper.

It is best to store a coin collection in a cool, dry environment. Of course, not everyone lives in such a climate. One common answer to this is to store a packet of silica gel in the same container as the coin collection. The gel is a desiccant and will absorb the moisture from the air. It can sometimes be obtained at photo shops, if not as easily through your local coin dealer.

Slabs

The word "slab" is numismatic slang for a tamper-resistant holder used to hold coins graded by third-party grading services. Third-party grading services came into existence to answer a market need particularly acute in the 1970s and early 1980s. Many investors became aware of the impressive track records of appreciation of certain coins. Coin values were generally on the rise, and the total population of people suddenly calling themselves coin dealers was on the rise too. Many of these new dealers had as their objective to actively promote coins as investments.

With so many inexperienced customers and dealers entering the market suddenly, it became apparent that there was a dearth of knowledge. While few in the investment market were concerned if the academic numismatic knowledge was being passed along, they were very concerned that the individual either selling them their investments or buying them back may be too inexperienced or too unscrupulous to properly grade the coins. Thus, a neutral arbiter was needed: the third-party grading service.

At left, PCGS "slab" of a 1927D 20-Dollar Gold Coin.
At right, NGC "slab" of a 1936 Buffalo Nickel

These firms examine coins and seal them in small transparent rectangular holders containing that firm's opinion of the grade. The holder does not damage the coin as embedding in Lucite would. The coin is fully removable, but any attempt to remove it will cause the holder to exhibit evidence of tampering, thus preventing anyone from switching a low-grade coin into a holder indicating a high grade.

There are obvious advantages to having someone without a vested interest in the answer determine the grade of a coin, but there are disadvantages as well. While the criteria applied to coin grading, particularly to United States and

Canadian coins are fairly clear and objective, no two coins wear in exactly the same manner and two individuals will not necessarily evaluate a coin in precisely the same manner.

It is quite common to send the same coin into different grading services and get significantly different answers. Sometimes this differs even in resubmitting the same coin to the same grading service. As a result, it has become common practice for dealers to review the lots of coins sent into the grading services on their return. Those coins graded too conservatively are usually broken out and resubmitted in hopes of achieving a higher grade. Those that received grades that the dealer believes to be higher than they would have assigned themselves are left in the holders and sold as third-party graded coins.

It is easy to see here that simply by means of attrition the population of third-party graded coins gradually becomes more and more skewed towards liberally graded coins. This does not mean that third-party coins are by definition misgraded, because there are always the "middle of the road" grades coming back from the services, which often are left intact, but it does mean that no collector (or investor or dealer) should blindly accept the grade printed on a plastic holder as gospel truth. There is no substitute for study, experience and examining enough coins to the point where you can make your own judgments.

There is nevertheless a market for "sight unseen" coins encapsulated in slabs. The values of such coins are determined by what the market perceives as the relative accuracy of the grading service in whose capsule the coin sits. The *Coin Dealer Newsletter* or "Graysheet" rates the relative merits of these grading services on a weekly basis. While most buyers do not pursue the sight unseen market, this quantifiable information is useful in determining which grading service to select for coins you are about to either buy or sell.

One outgrowth of the certified grading phenomenon is "population reports." Some services maintain a record of the quantity of specimens in each grade for each coin that passes through their hands. In theory this will indicate to the potential coin buyer how rarely a coin occurs in certain very high grades. These reports should be viewed with some caution. While it is officially expected that a dealer submitting a previously graded coin for regrading will indicate that it is the same coin, most do not. Hence, one specimen can easily end up on the population reports as two different coins.

A peculiar reaction to the proliferation of slabs is "slab aversion" by pure collectors who have no interest in investment. This author has seen and heard of numerous instances in which collectors have refused to buy needed coins at a grade and price that pleased them purely because the coins were in slabs. There is no logical support for such conduct, as obviously anyone who finds the holder odious can throw it away. This is a rare, but observed, fact.

Coin Collecting Online

It is entirely conceivable that in another few years one-third of all numismatic sales will be done over the Internet, yet at the moment, it is a secondary but growing market. Most dealers have constructed Web pages with varying results. Also, there are now a couple of services which consolidate a number of dealers' offerings into a series of pages in a common location for ease of searching. At the moment, both for the dealers and for the collectors in search of dealers, the "net" is still somewhat uncharted territory. It so far lacks some of the safety mechanisms that exist with periodicals or local shops. There are no customer service awards or standard policies for advertisers, nor are there local Better Business Bureaus to which one can appeal. This does not mean there are no means by which you can discern legitimate dealers from fly-by-nights. Many of the criteria you would apply to shop, mail order, and show dealers can be applied to net dealers. Many of the more serious dealers on the "Web" also have active advertising programs in conventional media, permitting you to check with those periodicals. Also, the importance of membership in a professional organization still applies. Ask how long the dealer has been in business, not just collecting coins as a hobbyist. Perhaps the most difficult part of selecting dealers on the Web is discerning who is a legitimate, full-time numismatic expert from the skilled home computer buff with the dream of becoming a real coin dealer.

Many auction sites take no responsibility for the transactions they host, but eBay, for example, does provide one way of screening out some of the worst offenders. Stars are used to indicate the amount of customer feedback the member has. Clicking on the star gives additional information such as whether any customers have left negative comments about their transactions. While even the most honest and knowledgeable dealer may not please everybody, a dealer with more than a few percent of their feedback listed as negative should be regarded with caution. A pair of sunglasses instead of a star indicates a new ID. Some unscrupulous dealers booted off eBay have been known to simply take new identities and start over.

Whatever the medium through which a collector seeks out dealers, a collector who is willing to do some research and ask the right questions is bound to end up with a few dealers in whom they can place confidence and find a certain level of comfort.

The Internet can be used for far more than purchases. E-mail is a wonderfully immediate way to correspond. Basic computer caution should be observed in order to avoid viruses. Never open an unexpected enclosure. Either ask the sender to post an image on a Web site, or verify that it was sent by someone you trust. Simply recognizing the return e-mail address is not enough as some viruses steal address books.

Ever more powerful search engines are making doing numismatic research a possibility. Unfortunately, too many collectors are confusing the somewhat random scattering of information on the Internet for a substitute for basic books. It does not even come close. All too often I have heard people say "I tried to look it up on the Internet and couldn't find it." This does not mean that the coin is rare. It more often means that the individual has spent hours using their computer when 10 minutes with a "Standard Catalog of World Coins" would have provided a simple answer, and more likely a more accurate one.

The thousands of numismatic Web sites are a great resource. Not only do the nation's most important numismatic organizations all have Web sites, but a large minority of local coin clubs do as well. Some can even be found through the ANA Web site itself. Discussion groups can also provide for interesting conversations normally only possible at larger coin shows. But remember, protect your security by not revealing an excess of personal information until you know well the trustworthiness of the individual to whom you are about to give your information. Never give out things such as passwords and home addresses. If you are convinced that a firm should be entrusted with your credit card number, send it to them in parts, contained in separate e-mails.

U.S. Government Web Sites

United States Mint: www.usmint.gov

Bureau of Engraving and Printing: www.moneyfactory.com

Coin Errors

An error is a coin manufactured incorrectly or one that is manufactured correctly on damaged or incorrectly made dies. Errors have been produced by a wide variety of mistakes, from the wrong metal being used, to the coin being struck off center. The Mint tries to prevent such coins from getting out. In most cases, error coins are usually caught and melted by the Mint.

Because the modern automated manufacturing process creates far fewer errors and greater uniformity than in ancient times, collectors of modern coins actually prize such mistakes. (Similar errors may actually reduce the value of ancient coins.) Errors in larger coins, proofs, and commemoratives tend to be scarcer because more attention is paid to the inspection process. Over the last 50 years, more have been getting out than in the past, and as a result, recent errors are not as valuable as early ones.

How each basic type of error occurs is explained following, along with what a typical example of such an error would retail for. Prices are for coins struck within the last 30 years. Coins may be worth more or less depending on the extent of the error. Values for most popular doubled-die cents appear in the regular listings.

1863 Indian Head Cent Struck Off Center

★ ★ COUNTERFEIT ALERT ★ ★

Most major doubled-die cents have been counterfeited. Virtually all examples of 1943 copper and 1944 steel cents are counterfeit. A magnet test will reveal deceptive plating, but not cleverly altered dates. Also, it is very easy to cause apparent errors by striking a coin with a coin or hammering foreign matter into it. Apparent off-metal strikes can simply be a coin plated after it was released from the Mint. Some very thin coins have been bathed in acid. (Is the surface abraded?) Clipped coins are easily confused for clip errors. Almost all two-headed American coins are concoctions. Do not presume a coin is a mint error until you determine how it was made. There are thousands of such "hoax coins" out there.

BIE Cent—A special kind of die chip in which a small chip out of the die between "B" and "E" in liberty looks like an extra letter "I." Fairly common in the 1950s.. **.25**

Blank—A blank, or planchet, is the piece of metal on which a coin is struck. Sometimes they escape the Mint with no processing whatsoever. Other times they escape unstruck, but do make it through the machine that upsets the edge slightly. These are called type I and type II blanks respectively.

Cent	.50	Nickel	2.50
Dime	2.00	Quarter	5.50
Half	17.00	Dollar	18.00

Brockage—Coin struck with a coin and a die instead of two dies. Caused by the previous coin adhering to one die. If it covers the whole die, it creates a "full brockage."

Cent	13.50	Nickel	35.00
Dime	45.00	Quarter	45.00
Half	250.00	Dollar	250.00

Clashed Dies—Coin struck with a die that has been previously struck by another die, leaving some of its impression behind. On the coin, the image of the primary die will be bold, and the image of the residual impression will be very faint.

Cent	.75	Nickel	1.00
Dime	1.75	Quarter	4.00
Half	12.00	Dollar	30.00

Clip (two types)—Coin struck on a blank that has part of its edge missing. There are two causes. A regular clip is caused by the punching device attempting to cut out the form of another coin before a previously punched blank is out of the way. A straight clip is caused when a blank is punched out from too near to the end of the sheet of metal.

Cent	.50	Nickel	2.50
Dime	2.00	Quarter	2.50
Half	10.00	Dollar	22.00

Susan B. Anthony Dollar with Cuds Caused by Major Die Breakage

Cud—A cud is a raised area of a coin near its edge. It is caused by a piece of the die chipping away. There is no striking surface in that spot to force the coin's metal down.

Cent	**1.00**	Nickel	**3.00**
Dime	**3.50**	Quarter	**6.50**
Half	**22.00**	Dollar	**35.00**

Die Chip—A die chip is similar to a cud, but it can be very small and occur anywhere in the die, not just the edge.

Cent	**.25 to 1.00**	Nickel	**.25 to 3.00**
Dime	**.50 to 3.00**	Quarter	**2.00 to 6.00**
Half	**5.00 to 20.00**	Dollar	**5.00 to 30.00**

Die Crack—A crack in the die will cause a very fine raised line across the surface of the coin it strikes. Larger cracks are worth more than values listed.

Cent	**.50**	Nickel	**.75**
Dime	**.75**	Quarter	**1.50**
Half	**2.50**	Dollar	**6.00**

Doubled Die—Caused by several reasons, all in the die manufacturing process. The coins will appear blurred at first glance, but upon inspection, the details will appear to be doubled.

Prices vary widely, from $10 to $500 or more.

This 1955 Doubled-Die Lincoln Cent is Worth up to $1,500 in Circulated Grades

1886 Double Struck Indian Head Cent

Double Struck—When a coin that has been struck fails to eject from between the pair of dies, it will receive a second impression, usually not centered.

Cent	10.00	Nickel	12.00
Dime	12.00	Quarter	40.00
Half	135.00	Dollar	400.00

Lamination—Occasionally called an "Occluded Gas Lamination," this error is caused by improper mixture of metal when the alloy is being made. It will appear as flaking on the surface.

Cent	.50	Nickel	3.00
Dime	4.00	Quarter	7.00
Half	12.00	Dollar	25.00

Mismatched Dies—This occurs when one of the two dies is intended for another coin. To date, all but one has been struck on a blank intended for the larger coin.

Cent and Dime	**two known**	Dollar and Quarter	**47,500.00**

1904 Indian Head Cent Struck Off Center

Off Center—When the blank is not lined up with the dies, only part of the impression is made. The other part of the blank remains just that—blank!

Cent	**1.00**	Nickel	**2.50**
Dime	**3.00**	Quarter	**8.00**
Half	**30.00**	Dollar	**40.00**

Struck Through—A coin that had foreign matter on the blank, which was impressed into the surface by the die.

Cent	**1.50**	Nickel	**1.50**
Dime	**1.50**	Quarter	**3.50**
Half	**9.00**	Dollar	**11.00**

New York Statehood Quarter Struck on a Dime Planchet

Wrong Metal—When a blank intended for one coin is accidentally mixed into blanks destined for another and is struck with those dies.

Cent	**100.00**	Nickel	**40.00**
Dime	**40.00**	Quarter	**45.00**
Half	**125.00**	Dollar	**375.00**

REGULAR MINT ISSUES

HALF CENTS

The half cent is far more popular today than it ever was when it actually circulated. While they permitted very precise dealings in commerce, they were still considered a nuisance by those who had to spend them. Demand for them was very small, mintages were low, and in some years none were struck for circulation at all. They were so low a priority that the Mint sometimes allocated no blanks for them, but struck them on second-hand merchant tokens instead. Even the banks didn't want them. From July 1811 until 1825 none were struck because of pressure from the banking industry. The half cent was finally abandoned in 1857.

Though not as popularly collected as the large cent, they are today considered scarce and desirable coins. Like the large cent, half cents are collected by die variety. Rare die combinations can be worth much more than common ones of the same year. Metal detector finds exhibiting porous surfaces are worth substantially less than the prices listed. Early dates are particularly difficult to find in better than well-worn condition, the Classic Head is much easier to find well preserved.

★ ★ COUNTERFEIT ALERT ★ ★

Cheap cast replicas of the 1793 exist, as do more dangerous counterfeits of that and the 1796 "no pole" variety. Authentic half cents exist with their dates skillfully altered to resemble the rare 1831 date. The 1840s proof restrikes were actually struck by the U.S. Mint in the 1850s and 1860s.

1795 Half Cent with Liberty Cap

LIBERTY CAP TYPE

	VG	VF		VG	VF
1793	4,000.00	10,000.00	1796, with pole	20,000.00	35,000.00
1794	800.00	2,200.00	1796, no pole	32,000.00	90,000.00
1795	570.00	1,500.00	1797	570.00	1,600.00

1800 Half Cent with Draped Bust

DRAPED BUST TYPE

	VG	VF		VG	VF
1800	75.00	300.00	1805	75.00	145.00
1802	1,600.00	8,000.00	1806	70.00	145.00
1803	70.00	275.00	1807	80.00	175.00
1804	70.00	150.00	1808	70.00	160.00
1804, spiked chin	90.00	175.00			

1825 Half Cent with Classic Head

CLASSIC HEAD TYPE

	VG	VF		VG	VF
1809	65.00	85.00	1831, restrike, *unc.*		6,500.00
1810	70.00	220.00	1832	65.00	95.00
1811	375.00	1,750.00	1833	65.00	95.00
1825	65.00	110.00	1834	65.00	95.00
1826	65.00	90.00	1835	65.00	95.00
1828	65.00	85.00	1836, *proof only*	—	6,000.00
1829	65.00	100.00	1836, restrike, *proof only*	—	20,000.00
1831	7,000.00	16,000.00			

1849 Half Cent with Braided Hair

BRAIDED HAIR TYPE

	VG	VF		VG	VF
1840, *proof only*	—	5,500.00	1842, *proof only*	—	6,000.00
1840, restrike, *proof only*	—	5,500.00	1842, restrike, *proof only*	—	6,000.00
1841, *proof only*	—	5,500.00	1843, *proof only*	—	6,500.00
1841, restrike, *proof only*	—	6,000.00	1843, restrike, *proof only*	—	6,000.00

	VG	VF		VG	VF
1844, *proof only*	—	6,000.00	1849, *proof only*	—	6,500.00
1844, restrike,			1849, restrike,		
proof only	—	6,000.00	*proof only*	—	6,000.00
1845, *proof only*	—	6,000.00	1849, large date	70.00	125.00
1845, restrike,			1850	60.00	125.00
proof only	—	6,000.00	1851	60.00	90.00
1846, *proof only*	—	6,000.00	1852, *proof only*	—	90,000.00
1846, restrike,			1852, restrike,		
proof only	—	6,000.00	*proof only*	—	5,000.00
1847, *proof only*	—	6,000.00	1853	75.00	115.00
1847, restrike,			1854	75.00	115.00
proof only	—	6,000.00	1855	75.00	125.00
1848, *proof only*	—	6,000.00	1856	75.00	125.00
1848, restrike,			1857	90.00	200.00
proof only	—	6,000.00			

LARGE CENTS

The United States large cent was a result of dual desires, one for a decimal coin worth one-hundredth of a dollar. The other was the need for a coin to replace British halfpennies and their imitations, which had been common in the American Colonies. It was slightly larger than the halfpenny, and the concept of decimal coinage was so innovative that the fraction "1/100" literally had to be written on the coin, along with the edge inscription "ONE HUNDRED FOR A DOLLAR."

The dies for striking early American coins had to be engraved by hand, and no two were identical. Because of this it has been very popular to collect them, especially the large cents, by die combination.

It is interesting to note that low mintages and mediocre acceptance by the public resulted in the very first large cents being little more than local Philadelphia coinage. Metal was in such short supply that junked copper hardware of inconsistent alloy was used for some early cents, giving a poor quality blank on which to strike the coin. People also resented the chain on the first design of 1793 as a symbol antithetical to liberty, and laughed at the frightened expression they perceived on the face of Miss Liberty. Later they became so popular that they were considered good luck. In the early 1800s, they were nailed to the rafters of new houses to bring good luck to its inhabitants. These old relics, found with characteristic square nail holes through them, have a discounted value but still hold historical interest for collectors, and have been given the nickname "rafter cents." Other large cents were stamped or hand engraved with advertising, personal initials, or risqué comments, then placed back into circulation.

During the 1850s, public irritation with the heaviness of the cent began to grow and, after eight years of research into smaller alternatives, the large cent was abandoned in 1857.

Because the hand-engraved dies with which these coins were struck have been individually identified, large cents are very actively collected by die variety. Rare die combinations can be worth much more than common ones of the same year. Metal detector finds exhibiting porous surfaces are worth substantially less than the prices listed. Early dates are particularly difficult to find in better than well-worn condition.

★ ★ COUNTERFEIT ALERT ★ ★

Large cents were not frequently counterfeited in their day. A few rarer dates were later counterfeited by casting (and possibly striking) to fool collectors. They include 1799, 1803, 1805 over 5, and 1851 over inverted 18. 1799 is also known altered from 1798. Some crude museum-souvenirs have been made of Chain Cents as well.

1793 Large Cent with Flowing Hair and Chain

1793 Large Cent with Flowing Hair and Wreath

FLOWING HAIR TYPE

	VG	VF
1793, chain rev.	11,000.00	30,000.00
1793, wreath rev.	2,500.00	8,000.00

1795 Large Cent with Liberty Cap (Double Struck and Rotated in Collar)

LIBERTY CAP TYPE

	VG	VF			VG	VF
1793	8,000.00	25,000.00		1795	500.00	1,200.00
1794	500.00	1,300.00		1796	500.00	1,500.00

1805 Large Cent with Draped Bust

DRAPED BUST TYPE

	VG	VF
1796	600.00	1,800.00
1797	175.00	450.00
1798	130.00	525.00
1799	5,000.00	17,000.00
1800	95.00	400.00
1801	85.00	360.00
1802	75.00	350.00
1803	80.00	350.00

	VG	VF
1804, original (open wreath)	2,000.00	5,000.00
1804, restrike (closed wreath), *unc.* —		1,500.00
1805	90.00	350.00
1806	95.00	400.00
1807	80.00	350.00

1809 Large Cent with Classic Head

CLASSIC HEAD TYPE

	VG	VF
1808	200.00	575.00
1809	350.00	1,300.00
1810	95.00	600.00
1811	175.00	1,000.00

	VG	VF
1812	85.00	525.00
1813	175.00	800.00
1814	90.00	530.00

1828 Large Cent with Coronet

CORONET TYPE

	VG	VF		VG	VF
1816	40.00	100.00	1827	35.00	75.00
1817, 13 stars	35.00	75.00	1828	35.00	90.00
1817, 15 stars	50.00	225.00	1829	35.00	100.00
1818	30.00	80.00	1830	35.00	90.00
1819	30.00	70.00	1831	35.00	80.00
1820	30.00	70.00	1832	35.00	80.00
1821	75.00	400.00	1833	35.00	80.00
1822	35.00	110.00	1834	35.00	80.00
1823	150.00	675.00	1835	35.00	80.00
1823, restrike	700.00	990.00	1836	35.00	80.00
1824	28.00	200.00	1837	30.00	80.00
1825	35.00	170.00	1838	30.00	80.00
1826	35.00	120.00	1839	40.00	90.00

1840 Large Cent with Braided Hair

	VG	VF		VG	VF
1840	30.00	50.00	1845	30.00	50.00
1841	30.00	50.00	1846	30.00	50.00
1842	30.00	50.00	1847	30.00	50.00
1843	30.00	50.00	1848	30.00	50.00
1844	30.00	50.00	1849	30.00	50.00

	VG	VF		VG	VF
1850	30.00	50.00	1854	30.00	50.00
1851	30.00	50.00	1855	30.00	50.00
1852	30.00	50.00	1856	30.00	50.00
1853	30.00	50.00	1857	125.00	225.00

FLYING EAGLE CENTS

After years of experimenting, the Mint introduced its new small cent in 1857. It was less than half the weight of the large cent, and was brown to beige in color due to its alloy of 88-percent copper and 12-percent nickel. It depicted an eagle flying left modeled after "Old Pete," a bird which years earlier had served as a mascot at the Mint. Initially these were released in certain quantities at *below face value* to encourage their acceptance, but the old large cents were so bulky that people didn't take long to convince. It's interesting to observe, in today's health-conscious atmosphere, that the wreath on the reverse contains, among other plants, tobacco.

The 1856 is technically a pattern but was widely distributed at the time, and is generally collected as part of the series.

★ ★ COUNTERFEIT ALERT ★ ★

Most of the 1856 cents encountered are counterfeit. They are usually made from authentic coins with the dates re-engraved.

1858 Flying Eagle Cent

	VG	VF		VG	VF
1856	7,300.00	12,500.00	1858, large letters	40.00	57.00
1857	39.00	50.00	1858, small letters	39.00	50.00

INDIAN HEAD CENTS

The origin of the Indian Head cent is one of the most charming in the field of numismatics. According to legend, James B. Longacre, engraver at the U.S. Mint, was entertaining an Indian chief who happened to be wearing his full war bonnet. As a gesture of whimsy, the chief removed his bonnet and placed it upon the head of Longacre's little girl, Sarah. The engraver instantly perceived that this was the image destined for the next American cent. Admittedly, fewer people believe this story as time goes on, but it does add a quaint bit of sentimentality to the origin of one of America's favorite coin designs.

When the Indian Head cent was first released, it was struck in the same copper-nickel alloy as the Flying Eagle cent. The reverse was a simple laurel wreath encircling the words "ONE CENT." The following year this was replaced by one of oak, often considered a symbol of authority, into the bottom of which was tied a bundle of arrows. Its top was open enough to fit a small American shield.

In 1864 nickel was removed from the alloy, giving the coin the bronze appearance that has since characterized the U.S. cent. It was also made thinner like our modern cent. This new bronze cent was very reminiscent in form to the private one-cent "Civil War Tokens," which were circulating at the time, and which cost a fraction of a cent to manufacture. The Mint was well aware of these obvious savings.

★ ★ COUNTERFEIT ALERT ★ ★

Struck counterfeits of 1867, 1868, 1873 open 3, and 1877 exist. Counterfeit 1908S and 1909S are often made by altering real 1908 and 1909 Indian cents.

1859 Copper-Nickel Alloy Indian Head Cent

COPPER-NICKEL ALLOY

	F	XF		F	XF
1859	23.00	120.00	1862	13.00	32.00
1860	22.00	75.00	1863	12.00	30.00
1861	45.00	120.00	1864	36.00	90.00

1882 Bronze Indian Head Cent

BRONZE

	F	XF		F	XF
1864	25.00	75.00	1881	7.00	22.00
1864, "L" on ribbon	130.00	280.00	1882	7.00	22.00
1865	18.00	45.00	1883	6.00	18.00
1866	75.00	200.00	1884	7.00	30.00
1867	90.00	200.00	1885	12.00	65.00
1868	70.00	180.00	1886	20.00	140.00
1869	235.00	455.00	1887	4.00	18.00
1870	235.00	415.00	1888	5.00	20.00
1871	285.00	460.00	1889	3.50	12.00
1872	380.00	630.00	1890	3.00	10.00
1873	60.00	175.00	1891	3.25	13.00
1874	42.00	115.00	1892	3.75	18.00
1875	55.00	125.00	1893	3.25	10.00
1876	70.00	240.00	1894	12.00	50.00
1877	1,600.00	2,850.00	1895	3.50	13.00
1878	65.00	250.00	1896	3.00	12.00
1879	16.00	75.00	1897	3.00	10.00
1880	8.00	29.00			

1902 Bronze Indian Head Cent

	F	XF		F	XF
1898	3.00	10.00	1905	2.50	9.00
1899	2.60	11.00	1906	2.50	9.00
1900	2.50	12.50	1907	2.50	8.00
1901	2.50	10.00	1908	2.50	9.00
1902	2.50	10.00	1908S	95.00	180.00
1903	2.50	10.00	1909	8.00	18.00
1904	2.50	10.00	1909S	575.00	750.00

LINCOLN CENTS

The Lincoln cent was the first regular issue United States coin to bear the portrait of a real person. It made its debut to celebrate the 100th year of Lincoln's birth. It was designed by a sculptor from outside the Mint's staff, Victor David Brenner. His initials are found prominently on the very first examples to be released. Some thought they were featured too prominently, and the outcry forced their removal, causing two varieties for the first year. Later, in 1918, they were added more discretely under the truncation of the shoulder.

Lincoln cents were a bronze alloy of 95-percent copper until 1943 when they were changed to zinc-coated steel to save copper for the war effort. Because some of them were confused with dimes they were replaced in 1944 and 1945 with cents made from melted spent shell casings, resulting in a much more conventional appearance. The original alloy was restored from 1946 until 1982 when it was finally abandoned for zinc plated with copper. This was to reduce the expense of manufacturing the cent. Many people don't realize it but if you cut one of the cents struck today in half it will not be orange or brown inside but white, revealing its true composition.

A new reverse was introduced in 1959 for the 150th anniversary of Lincoln's birth and the 50th anniversary of the Lincoln cent, depicting the

Lincoln Memorial in Washington, D.C.

In 2009, to commemorate the bicentennial of Lincoln's birth, the Mint struck four different reverse designs emblematic of various stages of Lincoln's life: (1) birth and early childhood in Kentucky, (2) formative years in Indiana, (3) professional life in Illinois, and (4) presidency.

The Lincoln cent is one of the most popularly collected coins on Earth. It is collected in most grades, and even the rarities can be found without too long a search.

★ ★ COUNTERFEIT ALERT ★ ★

The 1909S VDB, 1909S, 1914D, 1922-Plain, 1931S, and 1955 doubled dies have been extensively counterfeited. Most are altered cents of other dates. Counterfeits also exist of the 1972 doubled die. Virtually all 1943 bronze and 1944 steel cents are counterfeit. A magnet test will reveal the crudest counterfeits made by plating. Other 1943 bronze have been made by altering 1948 and by striking with false dies.

In addition to counterfeits, the collector should be aware of "reprocessed" cents. These are circulated 1943 steel cents given a fresh zinc coating to make them appear uncirculated. Many hobbyists are quite willing to have them in their collections, but it is important to know the difference. Don't look for luster, but look for traces of flatness at the cheekbone.

1909S VDB Lincoln Cent with Wheat Ears Reverse

WHEAT EARS REVERSE

	VF	MS-60		VF	MS-60
1909, VDB	13.00	14.00	1909S	165.00	310.00
1909S, VDB	1,100.00	1,500.00	1910	1.00	18.50
1909	3.50	15.50	1910S	25.00	82.50

	VF	MS-60
1911	2.50	20.00
1911D	15.50	85.00
1911S	38.00	170.00
1912	6.00	30.00
1912D	21.00	147.00
1912S	25.00	150.00
1913	3.50	35.00
1913D	10.50	90.00
1913S	25.00	200.00
1914	6.00	50.00
1914D	450.00	2,000.00
1914S	38.00	300.00
1915	15.00	90.00
1915D	6.50	70.00
1915S	30.00	170.00
1916	2.60	18.00
1916D	6.00	70.00

	VF	MS-60
1916S	7.50	80.00
1917	2.00	17.00
1917D	5.50	65.00
1917S	2.50	60.00
1918	1.30	13.00
1918D	5.50	70.00
1918S	4.00	65.00
1919	.75	9.00
1919D	4.20	55.00
1919S	2.70	45.00
1920	1.50	15.00
1920D	5.50	65.00
1920S	3.00	90.00
1921	3.00	42.00
1921S	6.00	110.00
1922D	25.00	95.00
1922, plain	1,450.00	9,000.00

1922 Plain (No D) Lincoln Cent with Wheat Ears Reverse

1932D Lincoln Cent with Wheat Ears Reverse

	VF	MS-60
1923	1.50	14.00
1923S	8.00	200.00
1924	1.25	21.00
1924D	60.00	235.00
1924S	5.00	115.00
1925	1.00	10.00
1925D	5.00	60.00
1925S	2.75	80.00
1926	.80	8.00
1926D	4.50	80.00
1926S	14.00	120.00
1927	.80	8.00
1927D	3.50	60.00
1927S	5.00	65.00
1928	.80	8.50
1928D	3.00	34.00
1928S	3.50	75.00
1929	1.00	6.00

	VF	MS-60
1929D	2.00	22.00
1929S	2.50	18.00
1930	1.25	4.00
1930D	1.25	12.00
1930S	1.00	10.00
1931	2.00	19.50
1931D	7.00	55.00
1931S	150.00	200.00
1932	3.50	19.50
1932D	3.00	18.00
1933	3.00	18.00
1933D	6.50	25.00
1934	.55	8.00
1934D	.95	26.50
1935	.50	4.50
1935D	.50	5.50
1935S	1.50	13.00
1936	.45	2.50
1936D	.45	3.75

1943 Lincoln Cents were produced with a zinc-coated steel during WWII

	VF	MS-60
1936S	.45	4.75
1937	.45	2.00
1937D	.45	2.50
1937S	.45	3.50
1938	.45	3.00
1938D	.55	3.70
1938S	.70	3.00
1939	.45	1.00
1939D	.60	2.50
1939S	.55	2.00
1940	.35	1.00
1940D	.35	1.25

	VF	MS-60
1940S	.35	1.50
1941	.35	1.00
1941D	.35	2.25
1941S	.50	2.75
1942	.35	.85
1942D	.35	.75
1942S	.70	4.50
1943, steel	.45	1.25
1943D, steel	.50	3.00
1943S, steel	.65	3.50
1944	.20	.65
1944D	.20	.65

	XF	MS-65
1944, D over S	120.00	400.00
1944S	.20	.65
1945	.20	.60
1945D	.20	.70
1945S	.20	.55
1946	.20	.55
1946D	.20	.50
1946S	.20	.60
1947	.15	.90
1947D	.15	.40
1947S	.20	.65
1948	.15	.65
1948D	.15	.65
1948S	.20	.75
1949	.15	.75
1949D	.15	.70
1949S	.20	1.00
1950	.15	.50
1950D	.15	.50
1950S	.15	.80
1951	.15	.90
1951D	.15	.60
1951S	.15	.75
1952	.15	.50
1952D	.15	.50
1952S	.15	1.20
1953	.15	.50
1953D	.15	.50
1953S	.15	.60
1954	.15	.75
1954D	.15	.50
1954S	.15	.50
1955	.15	.50
1955, doubled die	1,350.00	2,050.00
1955, minor date shift or "poor man's doubled die"	.20	1.20
1955D	.15	.50
1955S	.15	.70
1956	.15	.40
1956D	.15	.40
1957	.15	.40
1957D	.15	.40
1958	.15	.40
1958D	.15	.40

LINCOLN MEMORIAL REVERSE

	MS-65
1959	.50
1959D	.50
1960, large date	.50
1960, small date	7.00
1960D, large date	.30
1960D, small date	.30
1961	.30
1961D	.30
1962	.30
1962D	.30
1963	.30
1963D	.30
1964	.30
1964D	.30
1965	.30
1966	.30
1967	.50
1968	.30
1968D	.40
1968S	.40
1969	.60
1969D	.40
1969S	.40
1970	.40
1970D	.40
1970S, small date	55.00
1970S, large date	.20
1971	.35
1971D	.40
1971S	.25
1972	.25
1972, doubled die	800.00
1972D	.25
1972S	.25
1973	.25
1973D	.25
1973S	.25
1974	.25
1974D	.25
1974S	.25
1975	.25
1975D	.25

	MS-65		MS-65
1975S, *proof only*	5.50	1979D	.25
1976	.25	1979S, *proof only*	4.00
1976D	.25	1980	.25
1976S, *proof only*	5.00	1980D	.25
1977	.25	1980S, *proof only*	2.25
1977D	.25	1981	.25
1977S, *proof only*	3.00	1981D	.25
1978	.25	1981S, *proof only*	3.50
1978D	.25	1982	.25
1978S, *proof only*	3.00	1982D	.25
1979	.25	1982S, *proof only*	3.00

1982S Lincoln Cent with Lincoln Memorial Reverse

COPPER PLATED ZINC

	MS-65		MS-65
1982	.25	1983D	.50
1982D	.25	1983S, *proof only*	4.00
1983	.25	1984	.25
1983, doubled-die rev.	400.00	1984, doubled die	275.00

1990S Proof, Lincoln Cent Error (Coin Struck at San Francisco Mint without S Mark)

	MS-65		MS-65
1984D	.75	1996D	.25
1984S, *proof only*	4.50	1996S, *proof only*	6.50
1985	.25	1997	.25
1985D	.25	1997D	.25
1985S, *proof only*	6.00	1997S, *proof only*	11.50
1986	1.50	1998	.25
1986D	1.25	1998D	.25
1986S, *proof only*	7.50	1998S, *proof only*	9.50
1987	.25	1999	.25
1987D	.25	1999D	.25
1987S, *proof only*	5.00	1999S, *proof only*	5.00
1988	.25	2000	.15
1988D	.25	2000D	.15
1988S, *proof only*	4.00	2000S, *proof only*	4.00
1989	.25	2001	.25
1989D	.25	2001D	.25
1989S, *proof only*	6.00	2001S, *proof only*	5.00
1990	.25	2002	.25
1990D	.25	2002D	.25
1990S, *proof only*	5.00	2002S, *proof only*	4.00
1990S, w/o S *proof only*	2,750.00	2003	.25
1991	.25	2003D	.25
1991D	.25	2003S, *proof only*	4.00
1991S, *proof only*	5.00	2004	.25
1992	.25	2004D	.25
1992D	.25	2004S, *proof only*	4.00
1992S, *proof only*	5.00	2005	.25
1993	.25	2005D	.25
1993D	.25	2005S, *proof only*	4.00
1993S, *proof only*	7.00	2006	.25
1994	.25	2006D	.25
1994D	.25	2006S, *proof only*	4.00
1994S, *proof only*	4.00	2007	.25
1995	.25	2007D	.25
1995, doubled die	50.00	2007S, *proof only*	4.00
1995D	.25	2008	.25
1995S, *proof only*	9.50	2008D	.25
1996	.25	2008S, *proof only*	4.00

From left to right: (1) birth and early childhood in Kentucky, (2) formative years in Indiana, (3) professional life in Illinois, (4) and President.

TWO-CENT PIECES

Throughout the Civil War people hoarded coins, preferring to spend the less valuable private tokens and small denomination paper money than available. If the North fell, they thought that at least real coins would retain some value. A small change shortage resulted. The two-cent piece was introduced in an attempt to alleviate this shortage. It was the first coin to carry the inscription "In God We Trust."

These are usually found well worn, fewer than 1 in 100 surviving in Fine or better condition.

★ ★ COUNTERFEIT ALERT ★ ★

Counterfeits are not particularly common, though some scarce die-struck ones are known.

1871 Two-Cent Piece

	F	XF
1864, small motto (open D in God)	275.00	650.00
1864, large motto (narrow D in God)	25.00	44.00
1865	25.00	44.00
1866	25.00	44.00
1867	40.00	65.00
1868	40.00	65.00

	F	XF
1869	42.00	75.00
1870	50.00	120.00
1871	60.00	130.00
1872	500.00	960.00
1873, closed 3, *proof only*	—	2,200.00
1873, open 3, *proof restrike*	—	2,400.00

SILVER THREE-CENT PIECES

Different times have different priorities, and the reasons for striking coins in one era don't always seem to make sense to the people living in another. This is the case of the silver three-cent piece, often called the "trime." It and the three-dollar gold piece were issued to make it easier to purchase single and sheets of three-cent, first class postage stamps. Despite the extreme awkwardness of their small size, they were accepted enough in commerce that they continued to be struck in significant quantities for 12 years.

Its thinness prevented it from striking up well, and the Mint attempted to modify its design repeatedly. Getting a fully struck coin with no weak spots, even in higher grades, is truly difficult. Another problem resulting from their thinness was their frequent bending, dents and crinkling. Prices given are for flat, undamaged examples.

★ ★ COUNTERFEIT ALERT ★ ★

Counterfeits made to pass in circulation were struck in base silver and white metal for early dates, German silver (copper-nickel-zinc) dated 1860 and 1861. A struck counterfeit also exists for 1864.

1851O Silver Three-Cent Piece with No Border Around Star

NO BORDER AROUND STAR

	F	XF		F	XF
1851	45.00	75.00	1852	45.00	75.00
1851O	60.00	180.00	1853	45.00	75.00

TRIPLE BORDER AROUND STAR

	F	XF		F	XF
1854	50.00	110.00	1857	52.00	120.00
1855	80.00	215.00	1858	52.00	110.00
1856	52.00	120.00			

1863 Silver Three-Cent Piece with Double Border Around Star

DOUBLE BORDER AROUND STAR

	F	XF		F	XF
1859	55.00	90.00	1867	475.00	565.00
1860	50.00	90.00	1868	480.00	575.00
1861	50.00	90.00	1869	480.00	575.00
1862	60.00	100.00	1870	500.00	600.00
1863	400.00	500.00	1871	480.00	575.00
1864	400.00	500.00	1872	500.00	600.00
1865	475.00	565.00	1873, *proof only*	—	1,700.00
1866	400.00	520.00			

NICKEL THREE-CENT PIECES

The fact that the tiny silver three-cent piece survived at all indicated that there was some usefulness to that denomination, but its size was impractical. With Civil War silver hoarding occurring, the need for a convenient non-silver coin of this value was even more apparent. The three-cent coin was thus made bigger and changed to an alloy of 75-percent copper and 25-percent nickel, just enough nickel to give it a white color. Despite their active use in commerce for decades, they are not difficult to find well preserved.

★ ★ COUNTERFEIT ALERT ★ ★

Few if any counterfeits of this coin are known.

1865 Nickel Three-Cent Piece

	F	XF		F	XF
1865	20.00	37.00	1878, *proof only*	—	900.00
1866	20.00	37.00	1879	100.00	120.00
1867	20.00	37.00	1880	130.00	195.00
1868	20.00	37.00	1881	20.00	40.00
1869	20.00	40.00	1882	180.00	275.00
1870	22.50	42.00	1883	280.00	380.00
1871	24.00	43.00	1884	575.00	700.00
1872	25.00	45.00	1885	650.00	800.00
1873	25.00	45.00	1886, *proof only*	—	600.00
1874	25.00	45.00	1887	415.00	585.00
1875	30.00	50.00	1888	80.00	110.00
1876	30.00	55.00	1889	150.00	220.00
1877, *proof only*	—	2,550.00			

SHIELD NICKELS

The success of the 25-percent nickel, three-cent piece emboldened the Mint to strike a larger denomination in the same alloy the following year. Its design was an ornate shield, reminiscent of the then popular two-cent piece. One unfortunate characteristic of a coin struck in a hard alloy such as this is that its design is not always fully struck. In this case, not all of the horizontal shading lines are always clear, even on mint-state coins. In its second year of issue the design was simplified, with the rays between the stars on the reverse being removed.

★ ★ COUNTERFEIT ALERT ★ ★

Counterfeits intended to pass in circulation were struck bearing the dates 1870 to 1876.

1866 Shield Nickel with Rays

1867 Shield Nickel with No Rays

	F	XF		F	XF
1866, rays	55.00	175.00	1875	85.00	150.00
1867, rays	70.00	220.00	1876	75.00	135.00
1867	29.00	62.00	1877, *proof only*	—	3,000.00
1868	29.00	62.00	1878, *proof only*	—	1,750.00
1869	29.00	62.00	1879	620.00	750.00
1870	53.00	92.00	1880	800.00	1,300.00
1871	125.00	265.00	1881	450.00	625.00
1872	70.00	112.00	1882	29.00	62.00
1873, closed 3	65.00	145.00	1883	30.00	62.00
1873, open 3	55.00	82.50	1883, 3 over 2	400.00	800.00
1874	75.00	110.00			

LIBERTY NICKELS

The Liberty nickel had one of the most controversial beginnings of all American coins. The original design had the denomination of five cents indicated simply by the Roman numeral V, with the word cents simply understood, or so the Mint expected. However, some unprincipled persons gold plated these coins and passed them off as the new five-dollar coin. These plated frauds became known as racketeer nickels and prompted an immediate change in the coin's design. The word "cents" was added boldly underneath the large V. Today racketeer nickels have some value as collector's novelties, but not as much as a natural, unaltered coin. Interestingly, the original "no cents" nickel is quite common today in medium to high grades, perhaps as an evidence of it being considered a novelty in its day.

The famous 1913 Liberty nickel is not an authorized mint issue, but was struck at the U.S. Mint by a scheming employee with an eye to profit. Carefully marketed, the first advertisements to purchase these rare coins were placed by the original seller, knowing that no one else had any to sell, but knowing that this would excite interest in the numismatic community. Today, it is one of the most valuable coins in the world!

★ ★ COUNTERFEIT ALERT ★ ★

There are counterfeits of the 1913, but they are somewhat less dangerous as all five extant pieces are in known hands. 1912S pieces exist made from altered 1912D nickels.

1896 Liberty Nickel

	F	XF		F	XF
1883, no cents	7.00	10.00	1894	100.00	250.00
1883, with cents	45.00	90.00	1895	25.00	75.00
1884	45.00	98.00	1896	45.00	100.00
1885	900.00	1,400.00	1897	13.00	47.00
1886	425.00	725.00	1898	11.50	45.00
1887	35.00	85.00	1899	8.75	36.00
1888	75.00	200.00	1900	8.75	36.00
1889	35.00	85.00	1901	7.50	34.00
1890	30.00	70.00	1902	4.50	32.50
1891	25.00	65.00	1903	5.00	32.50
1892	25.00	70.00	1904	5.00	30.00
1893	25.00	68.00	1905	4.50	30.00

1907 Liberty Nickel

	F	XF		F	XF
1906	4.50	30.00	1911	4.50	30.00
1907	4.50	30.00	1912	4.50	30.00
1908	4.50	30.00	1912D	12.50	85.00
1909	4.50	30.00	1912S	300.00	950.00
1910	4.50	32.00	1913, *proof*	—	5,000,000.00

BUFFALO NICKELS

The Buffalo nickel, also called the Indian Head nickel, was one of the most artistically progressive American coins to have been struck when first issued. It was designed by James Earle Fraser, a noted sculptor of the era. Traditional belief holds that three different Indians posed for the obverse portrait, but this theory has recently been called into question. The original reverse depicting an American bison standing on a mound was changed for practical reasons the year it was issued, as the words "FIVE CENTS" were in such high relief that they would quickly wear off. The second reverse has the denomination in a recess below a plane on which the bison stands. The date is also rendered in high relief on these coins, and below Very Good usually wears off. Such dateless coins are of little value.

One entertaining sidelight to the Buffalo nickel is the Hobo nickel. This relic of American folk art consists of a Buffalo nickel with the portrait re-engraved by hand into a variety of different portraits. It was some individuals' way of fighting the poverty of the Great Depression, by making these works of art and selling them at a modest profit. Over the last few years they have come into their own and attempts to identify individual artists have met with some success.

★ ★ COUNTERFEIT ALERT ★ ★

The most famous counterfeit in the series is that of the three-legged Buffalo variety of 1937D. It should be noted that a real three-legged buffalo can be distinguished not simply because of its missing leg, but based on numerous minor details expected where the design meets the field that is missing as well. Other counterfeits are coins altered to appear as the 1913S Type II, 1918/7D, 1921S, 1924S, 1926D, and 1926S.

1913D Buffalo Nickel

	F	MS-60
1913, mound	12.00	35.00
1913D, mound	22.00	65.00
1913S, mound	50.00	130.00
1913, plain	12.50	35.00
1913D, plain	185.00	300.00
1913S, plain	450.00	900.00
1914	22.00	50.00
1914D	160.00	480.00
1914S	45.00	200.00

	F	MS-60
1915	8.00	52.00
1915D	45.00	225.00
1915S	105.00	625.00
1916	7.00	45.00
1916D	30.00	150.00
1916S	20.00	175.00
1917	8.00	60.00
1917D	55.00	400.00
1917S	80.00	455.00

1924 Buffalo Nickel

	F	MS-60
1918	8.00	110.00
1918, 8 over 7	2,950.00	30,000.00
1918D	65.00	470.00
1918S	55.00	550.00
1919	6.00	60.00

	F	MS-60
1919D	66.00	575.00
1919S	52.00	550.00
1920	3.50	60.00
1920D	37.00	565.00
1920S	30.00	525.00

	F	MS-60
1921	8.75	125.00
1921S	220.00	1,600.00
1923	4.50	65.00
1923S	27.00	600.00
1924	4.50	75.00
1924D	30.00	400.00
1924S	100.00	2,350.00
1925	3.75	42.00
1925D	40.00	390.00
1925S	17.50	450.00
1926	2.85	35.00
1926D	30.00	325.00
1926S	100.00	5,000.00
1927	2.50	35.00
1927D	8.00	160.00
1927S	6.00	485.00

	F	MS-60
1928	2.50	35.00
1928D	4.00	59.00
1928S	3.00	220.00
1929	2.50	35.00
1929D	3.00	55.00
1929S	2.25	48.00
1930	2.50	33.00
1930S	2.25	43.00
1931S	20.00	65.00
1934	2.50	50.00
1934D	4.75	83.00
1935	2.25	21.00
1935D	3.00	75.00
1935S	2.50	50.00
1936	2.25	16.00

1937D "Three-Legged" Buffalo

	F	MS-60
1936D	2.65	36.00
1936S	2.50	36.00
1937	2.25	15.00
1937D	2.50	30.00

	F	MS-60
1937D, three-legged	950.00	2,750.00
1937S	2.50	28.00
1938D	4.00	20.00
1938D, D over S	12.00	50.00

JEFFERSON NICKELS

The Jefferson nickel was the first circulating United States coin to be designed by public contest. Felix Schlag won $1,000 for his design featuring Jefferson's portrait on one side, and his home Monticello on the other. The initial rendition lacks the designer's initials, which were not added until 1966.

During World War II nickel was needed for the war effort, so from mid-1942 to the end of 1945, "nickels" were struck in an unusual alloy of 56-percent copper, 35-percent silver and nine-percent manganese. These "War Nickels" bear a large mintmark over the dome. These coins exhibit great brilliance when new, but quickly turn an ugly dull color with a moderate amount of wear.

A pair of special nickels were issued to circulation in 2004, struck to commemorate the bicentennial of the expedition of exploration, from St. Louis to the Pacific, led by Meriwether Lewis and William Clark. They bear the standard Jefferson obverse. One reverse bears clasped hands adapted from a Jefferson-era Indian peace medal. The other shows an old keelboat used for navigating rivers.

In 2005, another pair of special nickels commemorating Lewis and Clark's expedition were issued to circulation. One reverse depicts the American bison design similar to the Buffalo nickel. The other reverse design, called "Ocean in view!," was inspired by a journal entry from William Clark, documenting their view of the Pacific Ocean.

In 2006, the obverse was redesigned. The new image was based on an 1800 Rembrandt Peale portrait of Jefferson. 2006 also saw the return of the Monticello reverse, with more detail and relief to the design.

Due to the difficulty of getting the metal to flow into every crevice of the die, many coins are struck with the steps of Monticello on the standard reverse incompletely struck. Full step nickels sometimes command a premium from specialists.

★ ★ COUNTERFEIT ALERT ★ ★

1950D, crude casts were also made to circulate in the 1940s.

	VF	MS-65
1938	.80	4.00
1938D	1.25	3.50
1938S	2.50	4.75
1939	.25	1.75
1939D	6.00	110.00
1939S	1.50	30.00
1940	.30	4.00
1940D	.30	3.00
1940S	.30	5.00
1941	.25	3.00
1941D	.30	5.00
1941S	.30	5.00
1942	.25	6.00
1942D	3.00	50.00

WARTIME SILVER ALLOY

	VF	MS-65
1942P	1.50	14.00
1942S	2.00	15.00
1943P	1.50	9.00
1943P, 3 over 2	75.00	300.00
1943D	1.50	9.00
1943S	1.50	12.00
1944P	1.50	20.00
1944D	1.50	15.00
1944S	1.50	11.00
1945P	1.50	10.00
1945D	1.50	9.50
1945S	1.50	9.00

REGULAR ALLOY

	VF	MS-65
1946	.25	2.00
1946D	.25	1.85
1946S	.30	1.00
1947	.25	1.00
1947D	.25	1.20
1947S	.25	1.20
1948	.25	1.00
1948D	.25	2.20
1948S	.25	1.50
1949	.25	3.00
1949D	.30	1.75
1949D, D over S	40.00	210.00
1949S	.45	2.00
1950	.35	2.50
1950D	13.00	20.00
1951	.40	2.50
1951D	.40	4.00
1951S	.50	2.75

	VF	MS-65
1952	.25	2.00
1952D	.30	3.00
1952S	.25	1.00
1953	.25	1.00
1953D	.25	1.00
1953S	.25	1.00
1954	.25	1.00
1954D	.25	1.00
1954S	.25	1.50
1954S, S over D	14.00	50.00
1955	.40	1.00
1955D	—	.50
1955D, D over S	12.50	40.00
1956	—	.50
1956D	—	.50
1957	—	.50
1957D	—	.50
1958	—	.50
1958D	—	.50
1959	—	.30
1959D	—	.25
1960	—	.25
1960D	—	.25
1961	—	.25
1961D	—	.25
1962	—	.25
1962D	—	.25
1963	—	.25
1963D	—	.25
1964	—	.25
1964D	—	.25
1965	—	.25
1966	—	.25
1967	—	.25
1968D	—	.25
1968S	—	.25
1969D	—	.25
1969S	—	.25
1970D	—	.25
1970S	—	.25
1971	—	.75
1971D	—	.25
1971S, *proof only*	—	1.60
1972	—	.25
1972D	—	.25
1972S, *proof only*	—	2.00
1973	—	.25
1973D	—	.25

1965 Regular Alloy Jefferson Nickel

	MS-65			MS-65
1973S, *proof only*	—.....1.75	1980D	—.....25
1974	—.....25	1980S, *proof only*	—.....1.50
1974D	—.....25	1981P	—.....25
1974S, *proof only*	—.....2.00	1981D	—.....25
1975	—.....25	1981S, *proof only*	—.....2.00
1975D	—.....25	1982P	—.....2.00
1975S, *proof only*	—.....2.25	1982D	—.....1.25
1976	—.....25	1982S, *proof only*	—.....3.00
1976D	—.....25	1983P	—.....1.50
1976S, *proof only*	—.....2.00	1983D	—.....1.00
1977	—.....25	1983S, *proof only*	—.....4.00
1977D	—.....25	1984P	—.....1.25
1977S, *proof only*	—.....1.75	1984D	—.....25
1978	—.....25	1984S, *proof only*	—.....5.00
1978D	—.....25	1985P	—.....30
1978S, *proof only*	—.....1.75	1985D	—.....30
1979	—.....25	1985S, *proof only*	—.....4.00
1979D	—.....25	1986P	—.....30
1979S, *proof only*	—.....1.50	1986D	—.....1.00
1980P	—.....25		

2004D Jefferson Nickel with Peace Reverse

2004D Jefferson Nickel with Lewis and Clark Keelboat Reverse

	MS-65		MS-65
1986S, *proof only*	—......7.00	1993P	— 25
1987P	—.......25	1993D	— 25
1987D	—.......25	1993S, *proof only*	— 4.00
1987S, *proof only*	—......3.50	1994P	— 25
1988P	—.......25	1994P, matte finish	— ...75.00
1988D	—.......25	1994D	— 25
1988S, *proof only*	—......5.50	1994S, *proof only*	— 4.00
1989P	—.......25	1995P	— 25
1989D	—.......25	1995D	— 35
1989S, *proof only*	—......4.50	1995S, *proof only*	— 6.50
1990P	—.......25	1996P	— 25
1990D	—.......25	1996D	— 25
1990S, *proof only*	—......5.50	1996S, *proof only*	— 3.00
1991P	—.......25	1997P	— 25
1991D	—.......25	1997P, matte finish	— ...200.00
1991S, *proof only*	—......5.00	1997D	— 25
1992P	—.......75	1997S, *proof only*	— 5.00
1992D	—.......25	1998P	— 25
1992S, *proof only*	—......4.00	1998D	— 25

2005D Jefferson Nickel with Buffalo Reverse

2006D Jefferson Nickel with Large Head Facing Obverse/Enhanced Monticello Reverse

	MS-65		MS-65
1998S, *proof only* ..... — **4.50**		2004D, keelboat rev......... — ..... .35	
1999P......... — .... .25		2004S, keelboat rev., *proof only* ... **8.00**	
1999D .... — .... .25		2005P, Buffalo rev......... — ..... .35	
1999S, *proof only* ..... — **3.50**		2005D, Buffalo rev. .... — ..... .35	
2000P........ — .... .25		2005S, Buffalo rev., *proof only* — **8.00**	
2000D .... — .... .25		2005P, Pacific Coastline rev.... — ..... .35	
2000S, *proof only* ..... — **2.00**		2005D, Pacific Coastline rev.... — ..... .35	
2001P........ — .... .30		2005S, Pacific Coastline rev.,	
2001D .... — .... .30		*proof only* .... — **7.00**	
2001S, *proof only* ..... — **2.00**		2006P, Large head facing/enhanced	
2002P........ — .... .25		Monticello........ — ..... .35	
2002D .... — .... .25		2006D, Large head facing/enhanced	
2002S, *proof only* ..... — **2.00**		Monticello........ — ..... .35	
2003P........ — .... .30		2006S, Large head facing/enhanced	
2003D .... — .... .30		Monticello, *proof only*.... — **6.00**	
2003S, *proof only* ..... — **2.00**		2007P .... — ..... .35	
2004P, peace rev. ..... — .... .35		2007D .... — ..... .35	
2004D, peace rev...... — .... .35		2007S, obv., *proof only* ..... — **6.00**	
2004S, peace rev.,		2008P .... — ..... .35	
proof only .... — **8.00**		2008D........ — ..... .35	
2004P, keelboat rev. .... — .... .35		2008S, obv., *proof only* ..... — **6.00**	

BUST HALF DIMES

The United States did not always have nickel five-cent pieces. The original ones were very small silver coins called half dimes. Their designs almost always resembled those used on large whole dimes. Despite it being a priority of George Washington, half dimes were not consistently struck in early America. Between 1805 and 1829 none were struck at all.

The bust half dime's thinness resulted in frequent bending and dents. Prices given are for flat, undamaged examples. Rare die combinations of early specimens command a premium from specialists.

1794 Half Dime with Flowing Hair

1796 Half Dime with Draped Bust and Small Eagle

FLOWING HAIR TYPE

	VG	VF
1794	1,400.00	2,800.00
1795	1,100.00	2,400.00

DRAPED BUST/SMALL EAGLE

	VG	VF
1796	1,500.00	3,500.00
1797	1,300.00	3,250.00

1800 Half Dime with Draped Bust and Heraldic Eagle

1829 Half Dime with Capped Bust

DRAPED BUST/HERALDIC EAGLE		
	VG	VF
1800	900.00	2,500.00
1801	950.00	2,800.00
1802	27,000.00	65,000.00
1803	990.00	2,500.00
1805	1,300.00	3,000.00

CAPPED BUST TYPE		
	VG	VF
1829	55.00	110.00
1830	45.00	95.00
1831	45.00	95.00
1832	45.00	95.00
1833	45.00	95.00
1834	45.00	95.00
1835	45.00	95.00
1836	45.00	98.00
1837	50.00	110.00

SEATED LIBERTY HALF DIMES

Following the introduction of the Seated Liberty design by Christian Gobrecht on the silver dollar, the smaller coins were gradually brought into harmony with this design. It is generally accepted that the seated goddess version of Liberty was directly or indirectly inspired by depictions of the Roman allegory of Britannia on British coins. The half dime and dime, because of their small size, were redesigned to have a laurel wreath encircling the denomination on the reverse, rather than an eagle.

There were several minor changes over the life of this coin. After only a year the plain obverse was ornamented by 13 stars. Two years later additional drapery was added below Liberty's elbow. The arrows by the date from 1853 to 1855 indicate a 7-1/2-percent reduction in weight. A far more obvious design change was the shift of the words "UNITED STATES OF AMERICA" from the reverse to the obverse in 1860.

The seated half dime's thinness resulted in frequent bending and dents. Prices given are for flat, undamaged examples.

★ ★ COUNTERFEIT ALERT ★ ★

Counterfeit half dimes are not frequently encountered.

1837 Seated Liberty Half Dime with Plain Obverse Field

SEATED LIBERTY—
PLAIN OBVERSE FIELD

	VG	VF		VG	VF
1837	42.00	120.00	1838O	150.00	475.00

1855O Seated Liberty Half Dime with Stars and Arrows on Obverse

SEATED LIBERTY—
STARS ON OBVERSE

	VG	VF		VG	VF
1838	20.00	30.00	1840O	30.00	70.00
1839	20.00	35.00	1841	17.50	30.00
1839O	30.00	50.00	1841O	22.00	55.00
1840	20.00	40.00	1842	20.00	35.00

	VG	VF		VG	VF
1842O	45.00	250.00	1852O	45.00	145.00
1843	20.00	35.00	1853, no arrows	50.00	145.00
1844	20.00	35.00	1853O, no arrows	325.00	850.00
1844O	105.00	450.00	1853, arrows	20.00	35.00
1845	20.00	35.00	1853O, arrows	20.00	35.00
1846	550.00	1,250.00	1854	20.00	35.00
1847	20.00	35.00	1854O	20.00	35.00
1848	20.00	35.00	1855	20.00	35.00
1848O	25.00	65.00	1855O	22.00	55.00
1849	20.00	60.00	1856	20.00	35.00
1849, overdates	26.00	62.00	1856O	20.00	60.00
1849O	40.00	225.00	1857	20.00	35.00
1850	20.00	40.00	1857O	20.00	45.00
1850O	25.00	70.00	1858	20.00	35.00
1851	20.00	35.00	1858O	20.00	45.00
1851O	20.00	45.00	1859	20.00	45.00
1852	20.00	35.00	1859O	21.00	48.00

1863 Seated Liberty Half Dime with Legend on Obverse

SEATED LIBERTY— LEGEND ON OBVERSE

	VG	VF		VG	VF
1860	20.00	35.00	1867S	40.00	90.00
1860O	20.00	35.00	1868	90.00	220.00
1861	20.00	35.00	1868S	25.00	45.00
1862	30.00	60.00	1869	25.00	45.00
1863	250.00	400.00	1869S	22.00	42.00
1863S	45.00	95.00	1870	22.00	42.00
1864	475.00	800.00	1870S		unique
1864S	75.00	200.00	1871	20.00	40.00
1865	475.00	750.00	1871S	30.00	70.00
1865S	40.00	90.00	1872	20.00	40.00
1866	475.00	700.00	1872S	20.00	40.00
1866S	40.00	90.00	1873	20.00	40.00
1867	650.00	900.00	1873S	25.00	40.00

BUST DIMES

Due to limited mint capacity dimes were not struck until 1796, even though other denominations of United States silver were struck two years earlier. Dime production was suspended occasionally when enough small Mexican coins were imported to satisfy demand. The initial reverse design, which showed a rather skinny eagle within a wreath, was replaced after two more years with a plumper eagle carrying a heraldic shield. In 1809 a cap was added to Liberty, and her bust was turned to the left. That same year a denomination first appeared, not as "dime," but as "10C." Rare die combinations of early specimens command a premium from specialists.

★ ★ COUNTERFEIT ALERT ★ ★

Scarce cast counterfeits are known.

1796 Dime with Draped Bust and Small Eagle

DRAPED BUST/SMALL EAGLE

	VG	VF
1796	2,000.00	3,500.00
1797, 13 stars	2,000.00	3,500.00
1797, 16 stars	2,000.00	3,500.00

1807 Dime with Draped Bust and Heraldic Eagle

DRAPED BUST/HERALDIC EAGLE

	VG	VF		VG	VF
1798, over 97, 13 stars	3,000.00	7,000.00	1803	800.00	1,800.00
1798, over 97, 16 stars	850.00	1,700.00	1804, 13 stars	1,900.00	5,500.00
1798	900.00	2,000.00	1804, 14 stars	2,100.00	6,000.00
1800	850.00	1,800.00	1805	700.00	1,300.00
1801	900.00	2,500.00	1807	700.00	1,300.00
1802	1,400.00	3,200.00			

1830/29 Dime with Capped Bust

CAPPED BUST TYPE

	VG	VF		VG	VF
1809	250.00	800.00	1828, large date	110.00	375.00
1811, over 9	200.00	650.00	1828, small date	45.00	195.00
1814, small date	70.00	400.00	1829, (varieties)	40.00	80.00
1814, large date	40.00	200.00	1830, 30 over 29	60.00	250.00
1820	40.00	150.00	1830	40.00	80.00
1821, small date	40.00	175.00	1831	40.00	80.00
1821, large date	40.00	150.00	1832	40.00	80.00
1822	625.00	1,700.00	1833	40.00	80.00
1823, 3 over 2	40.00	150.00	1834	40.00	80.00
1824, 4 over 2	50.00	400.00	1835	40.00	80.00
1825	40.00	150.00	1836	40.00	80.00
1827	40.00	140.00	1837	40.00	80.00

SEATED LIBERTY DIMES

Following the introduction of the Seated Liberty design by Christian Gobrecht on the silver dollar, the smaller coins were gradually brought into harmony with this design. It is generally accepted that the seated goddess version of Liberty was directly or indirectly inspired by depictions of the Roman allegory of Britannia on British coins. The dime and half dime, because of their small size, were redesigned to have a laurel wreath encircling the denomination on the reverse, rather than an eagle.

There were several minor changes over the life of this coin. After somewhat more than a year the plain obverse was ornamented by 13 stars. A year later, additional drapery was added below Liberty's elbow. The arrows by the date from 1853 to 1855 indicate a seven-percent reduction in weight, those in 1873 and 1874 saw a minuscule increase. A far more obvious design change was the shift of the words "UNITED STATES OF AMERICA" from the reverse to the obverse in 1860.

The seated dime's thinness resulted in frequent bending and dents. Prices given are for flat, undamaged examples.

★ ★ COUNTERFEIT ALERT ★ ★

Collector counterfeits of seated dimes are not frequently encountered, but circulating counterfeits were struck in copper, lead, and white metal (tin and lead alloys), particularly during the 1850s-1860s.

1837 Seated Liberty Dime with Plain Obverse Field

**SEATED LIBERTY—
OBVERSE FIELD PLAIN**

	VG	VF		VG	VF
1837	50.00	300.00	1838O	75.00	400.00

1844 Seated Liberty Dime with Stars on Obverse

SEATED LIBERTY—
STARS ON OBVERSE

	VG	VF		VG	VF
1838, (varieties)	20.00	45.00	1850O	27.00	90.00
1839	20.00	45.00	1851	25.00	35.00
1839O	22.50	60.00	1851O	25.00	90.00
1840	20.00	45.00	1852	20.00	32.00
1840O	22.50	70.00	1852O	30.00	125.00
1840, extra drapery			1853, no arrows	110.00	275.00
from elbow	50.00	200.00	1853, arrows	18.00	30.00
1841	20.00	32.00	1853O, arrows	20.00	45.00
1841O	22.00	45.00	1854	20.00	30.00
1842	20.00	32.00	1854O	20.00	30.00
1842O	23.00	75.00	1855	20.00	30.00
1843	20.00	32.00	1856	20.00	35.00
1843O	70.00	325.00	1856O	20.00	35.00
1844	350.00	800.00	1856S	225.00	550.00
1845	20.00	32.00	1857	20.00	35.00
1845O	35.00	250.00	1857O	20.00	35.00
1846	300.00	850.00	1858	20.00	35.00
1847	25.00	85.00	1858O	25.00	90.00
1848	21.50	55.00	1858S	200.00	475.00
1849	20.00	40.00	1859	20.00	45.00
1849O	30.00	135.00	1859O	20.00	45.00
1850	25.00	35.00	1859S	225.00	550.00
			1860S	55.00	145.00

SEATED LIBERTY—
LEGEND ON OBVERSE

	VG	VF		VG	VF
1860	22.00	36.00	1860O	600.00	1,950.00

1877 Seated Liberty Dime with Legend on Obverse

	VG	VF		VG	VF
1861	20.00	35.00	1874S, arrows	70.00	160.00
1861S	90.00	275.00	1875	20.00	30.00
1862	20.00	35.00	1875CC	20.00	30.00
1862S	65.00	185.00	1875S	20.00	30.00
1863	500.00	900.00	1876	20.00	30.00
1863S	55.00	145.00	1876CC	20.00	30.00
1864	500.00	750.00	1876S	20.00	30.00
1864S	45.00	110.00	1877	20.00	30.00
1865	575.00	875.00	1877CC	20.00	40.00
1865S	55.00	135.00	1877S	20.00	30.00
1866	600.00	950.00	1878	20.00	30.00
1866S	65.00	150.00	1878CC	90.00	225.00
1867	700.00	1,100.00	1879	310.00	450.00
1867S	60.00	150.00	1880	275.00	375.00
1868	22.00	40.00	1881	300.00	425.00
1868S	35.00	85.00	1882	20.00	30.00
1869	35.00	80.00	1883	20.00	30.00
1869S	30.00	55.00	1884	20.00	30.00
1870	22.00	40.00	1884S	35.00	65.00
1870S	375.00	650.00	1885	20.00	30.00
1871	20.00	33.00	1885S	650.00	1,750.00
1871CC	3,500.00	8,500.00	1886	20.00	30.00
1871S	55.00	130.00	1886S	70.00	125.00
1872	20.00	30.00	1887	20.00	30.00
1872CC	1,100.00	3,000.00	1887S	20.00	30.00
1872S	60.00	150.00	1888	20.00	30.00
1873, closed 3	20.00	30.00	1888S	20.00	30.00
1873, open 3	30.00	50.00	1889	20.00	30.00
1873CC		unique	1889S	20.00	45.00
1873, arrows	20.00	60.00	1890	20.00	30.00
1873CC, arrows	3,000.00	6,000.00	1890S	20.00	50.00
1873S, arrows	30.00	70.00	1891	20.00	30.00
1874, arrows	30.00	50.00	1891O	20.00	30.00
1874CC, arrows	6,500.00	12,500.00	1891S	18.00	30.00

BARBER DIMES

The dime, quarter, and half dollar introduced in 1892 bear a portrait head of Liberty instead of an entire figure. They were designed by Chief Engraver Charles E. Barber, after whom they have been popularly named. More practical than artistically adventurous, contemporaries thought the design rather boring if not unpleasant. Because of its small size, the dime differed from the other two denominations in the Barber series in that the reverse simply has the value within a wreath, rather than an eagle, much as occurred with the Seated Liberty coinage.

★ ★ COUNTERFEIT ALERT ★ ★

The rare 1894S has been counterfeited.

1898S Barber Dime

	F	XF		F	XF
1892	16.00	28.00	1896O	300.00	480.00
1892O	32.00	75.00	1896S	280.00	400.00
1892S	200.00	300.00	1897	8.00	33.00
1893, 3 over 2	175.00	300.00	1897O	280.00	480.00
1893	20.00	46.00	1897S	96.00	185.00
1893O	110.00	200.00	1898	8.00	32.50
1893S	38.00	85.00	1898O	85.00	205.00
1894	115.00	200.00	1898S	32.00	80.00
1894O	205.00	445.00	1899	7.50	26.00
1894S, *very rare proof*		1,300,000.00	1899O	70.00	150.00
1895	300.00	575.00	1899S	26.00	48.00
1895O	880.00	2,500.00	1900	7.00	28.00
1895S	130.00	240.00	1900O	110.00	225.00
1896	55.00	98.00	1900S	12.50	32.00

	F	XF
1901	6.50	27.50
1901O	16.00	67.50
1901S	360.00	520.00
1902	5.50	23.00
1902O	15.00	62.50
1902S	55.00	135.00
1903	4.50	25.00
1903O	13.50	50.00
1903S	340.00	800.00
1904	6.00	25.00
1904S	160.00	350.00
1905	6.00	25.00
1905O	35.00	98.00
1905S	9.00	45.00
1906	4.00	25.00
1906D	8.00	37.00
1906O	48.00	98.00
1906S	12.00	48.00
1907	4.00	25.00
1907D	8.50	46.00
1907O	32.00	63.00
1907S	16.00	67.50
1908	4.00	25.00
1908D	6.00	30.00

	F	XF
1908O	42.50	98.00
1908S	11.50	48.00
1909	4.00	25.00
1909D	60.00	135.00
1909O	12.50	50.00
1909S	85.00	190.00
1910	4.00	25.00
1910D	8.50	48.00
1910S	50.00	110.00
1911	4.00	25.00
1911D	4.00	25.00
1911S	8.50	41.50
1912	4.00	25.00
1912D	4.00	25.00
1912S	6.00	34.00
1913	4.00	25.00
1913S	85.00	240.00
1914	4.00	25.00
1914D	4.00	25.00
1914S	8.00	42.00
1915	4.00	25.00
1915S	32.50	70.00
1916	4.00	25.00
1916S	4.50	25.00

MERCURY DIMES

The name Mercury for this dime is a misnomer. Designed by Adolph Weinman, it actually depicts Liberty wearing a winged cap, representing freedom of thought. It was received with wide acclaim for its artistic merit when it was first released as part of a program for the beautification of United States coinage. The reverse carries the ancient Roman fasces, a symbol of authority still seen in the United States Senate. The horizontal bands tying the fasces together do not always strike up distinctly from each other, and those coins with "full split bands" often command a premium.

★ ★ COUNTERFEIT ALERT ★ ★

These include 1916D, 1921, 1921D, 1931D, 1942/1, 1942/1D, most of which have been made by altering the mintmark on a more common date. The date 1923D is a fantasy, as it wasn't struck.

1916D Mercury Dime

	VF	MS-60		VF	MS-60
1916	7.00	33.00	1919S	17.00	190.00
1916D	4,200.00	14,000.00	1920	4.00	27.50
1916S	15.00	46.00	1920D	8.00	115.00
1917	5.50	30.00	1920S	8.00	115.00
1917D	26.00	140.00	1921	280.00	1,175.00
1917S	6.50	64.00	1921D	400.00	1,325.00
1918	12.00	70.00	1923	4.00	27.50
1918D	12.00	110.00	1923S	18.00	165.00
1918S	10.00	100.00	1924	4.50	45.00
1919	5.50	38.00	1924D	22.00	175.00
1919D	25.00	190.00	1924S	12.00	170.00

1942 Mercury Dime, 2 over 1

	VF	MS-60
1925	4.00	28.00
1925D	44.00	370.00
1925S	14.00	190.00
1926	3.00	25.00
1926D	9.90	125.00
1926S	70.00	900.00
1927	3.50	27.00
1927D	24.00	200.00
1927S	9.00	290.00
1928	3.50	27.50
1928D	22.00	200.00
1928S	6.50	125.00
1929	3.00	24.00
1929D	8.00	28.00
1929S	5.00	32.50
1930	3.75	26.00
1930S	7.00	82.00
1931	4.50	35.00
1931D	18.00	98.00

	VF	MS-60
1931S	11.00	96.00
1934	3.00	30.00
1934D	7.50	50.00
1935	3.00	11.00
1935D	6.50	38.00
1935S	3.00	25.00
1936	3.00	10.00
1936D	4.20	28.00
1936S	3.00	20.00
1937	2.50	9.00
1937D	3.00	24.00

	VF	MS-60
1937S	3.00	23.00
1938	2.50	14.00
1938D	5.00	18.00
1938S	3.25	21.00
1939	2.50	10.00
1939D	2.50	8.00
1939S	3.00	25.00
1940	3.00	7.00

	VF	MS-60
1940D	3.00	8.00
1940S	3.00	9.00
1941	3.00	7.00
1941D	3.00	7.00
1941S	3.00	8.00
1942, 2 over 1	750.00	2,250.00
1942D, 2 over 1	840.00	2,650.00
1942	3.00	7.00
1942D	3.00	8.00
1942S	3.00	9.50

	VF	MS-60
1943	3.00	7.00
1943D	3.00	7.50
1943S	3.00	9.00
1944	3.00	7.00
1944D	3.00	7.50
1944S	3.00	7.50
1945	3.00	7.00
1945D	3.00	7.00
1945S	3.00	7.00
1945S, micro S	9.00	60.00

ROOSEVELT DIMES

The fact that the dime was chosen to bear the image of Franklin Roosevelt is not a coincidence. It was selected to remind people of the president's involvement in the March of Dimes, as he himself was crippled by polio. The coin was designed on a tight deadline by Chief Engraver John R. Sinnock. There are no true rarities in this series.

★ ★ COUNTERFEIT ALERT ★ ★

Counterfeit Roosevelt dimes are quite rare.

1964 Roosevelt Dime (Silver)

	XF	MS-65		XF	MS-65
1946	2.00	4.50	1948S	2.00	7.00
1946D	2.00	4.50	1949	3.00	35.00
1946S	2.00	4.50	1949D	2.00	14.00
1947	2.00	7.00	1949S	7.50	50.00
1947D	2.00	8.00	1950	2.25	16.00
1947S	2.00	6.00	1950D	2.00	7.00
1948	2.00	6.00	1950S	3.75	50.00
1948D	2.00	9.00	1950S, S over D	70.00	225.00

1968 Roosevelt Dime (Cupro-Nickel Clad Copper)

	XF	MS-65
1951	2.00	4.00
1951D	2.00	3.50
1951S	3.00	18.00
1952	2.00	3.50
1952D	2.00	3.50
1952S	2.00	6.00
1953	2.00	3.50
1953D	2.00	3.50
1953S	2.00	3.50
1954	2.00	3.50
1954D	2.00	3.50
1954S	2.00	3.50
1955	2.00	3.50
1955D	2.00	3.50
1955S	2.00	3.50
1956	—	3.00
1956D	—	3.00

	XF	MS-65
1957	—	2.50
1957D	—	2.50
1958	—	2.30
1958D	—	2.30
1959	—	2.30
1959D	—	2.30
1960	—	2.30
1960D	—	2.30
1961	—	2.30
1961D	—	2.30
1962	—	2.30
1962D	—	2.30
1963	—	2.00
1963D	—	2.00
1964	—	2.00
1964D	—	2.00

CUPRO-NICKEL CLAD COPPER

		MS-65
1965	—	.60
1966	—	.50
1967	—	.75
1968	—	.50
1968D	—	.50
1968S, *proof only*	—	1.50
1969	—	.50
1969D	—	.50
1969S, *proof only*	—	1.50
1970	—	.50
1970D	—	.50
1970S, *proof only*	—	1.50
1971	—	.50
1971D	—	.50

		MS-65
1971S, *proof only*	—	1.50
1972	—	.50
1972D	—	.50
1972S, *proof only*	—	1.50
1973	—	.50
1973D	—	.50
1973S, *proof only*	—	1.50
1974	—	.50
1974D	—	.50
1974S, *proof only*	—	1.50
1975	—	.50
1975D	—	.50
1975S, *proof only*	—	2.25
1976	—	.75

	MS-65
1976D	— .50
1976S, *proof only*	— 1.50
1977	— .50
1977D	— .50
1977S, *proof only*	— 2.25
1978	— .50
1978D	— .50
1978S, *proof only*	— 1.50
1979	— .50
1979D	— .50
1979, thick S, *proof only*	— 1.50
1979, thin S, *proof only*	— 2.25
1980P	— .50
1980D	— .50
1980S, *proof only*	— 1.50
1981P	— .50
1981D	— .50
1981S, *proof only*	— 1.50
1982P	— 3.50
1982, no mintmark error	80.00 200.00
1982D	— .50
1982S, *proof only*	— 1.50
1983P	— .50
1983D	— .50
1983S, *proof only*	— 1.50
1984P	— .50
1984D	— .50
1984S, *proof only*	— 2.00
1985P	— .50
1985D	— .50
1985S, *proof only*	— 1.50
1986P	— .50
1986D	— .50
1986S, *proof only*	— 2.75
1987P	— .50
1987D	— .50
1987S, *proof only*	— 1.50
1988P	— .50
1988D	— .50
1988S, *proof only*	— 3.00
1989P	— .50
1989D	— .50
1989S, *proof only*	— 4.00
1990P	— .50
1990D	— .50
1990S, *proof only*	— 2.00
1991P	— .50
1991D	— .50

	MS-65
1991S, *proof only*	— 3.00
1992P	— .50
1992D	— .50
1992S, *proof only*	— 4.00
1992S, Silver, *proof only*	— 5.00
1993P	— .50
1993D	— .50
1993S, *proof only*	— 5.00
1993S, Silver, *proof only*	— 8.50
1994P	— .50
1994D	— .50
1994S, *proof only*	— 5.00
1994S, Silver, *proof only*	— 8.50
1995	— .50
1995D	— .50
1995S, *proof only*	— 18.00
1995S, Silver, *proof only*	— 25.00
1996	— .50
1996D	— .50
1996W	— 14.00
1996S, *proof only*	— 2.50
1996S, Silver, *proof only*	— 8.50
1997P	— .50
1997D	— .50
1997S, *proof only*	— 11.00
1997S, Silver, *proof only*	— 25.00
1998P	— .50
1998D	— .50
1998S, *proof only*	— 4.00
1998S, Silver, *proof only*	— 8.00
1999P	— .50
1999D	— .50
1999S, *proof only*	— 4.00
1999S, Silver, *proof only*	— 6.50
2000P	— .50
2000D	— .50
2000S, *proof only*	— 1.00
2000S, Silver, *proof only*	— 4.50
2001P	— .50
2001D	— .50
2001S, *proof only*	— 1.50
2001S, Silver, *proof only*	— 5.00
2002P	— .50
2002D	— .50
2002S, *proof only*	— 1.00
2002S, Silver, *proof only*	— 5.50
2003P	— .50
2003D	— .50

	MS-65			MS-65
2003S, *proof only*	—	.2.00	2006D	—	.50
2003S, Silver, *proof only*	—	.4.00	2006S, *proof only*	—	.4.75
2004P	—	.50	2006S, Silver, *proof only*	—	.4.00
2004D	—	.50	2007P	—	.50
2004S, *proof only*	—	.4.75	2007D	—	.50
2004S, Silver, *proof only*	—	.4.00	2007S, *proof only*	—	.4.75
2005P	—	.50	2007S, Silver, *proof only*	—	.4.00
2005D	—	.50	2008P	—	.50
2005S, *proof only*	—	.2.25	2008D	—	.50
2005S, Silver, *proof only*	—	.4.00	2008S, *proof only*	—	.5.00
2006P	—	.50	2008S, Silver, *proof only*	—	.4.25

TWENTY-CENT PIECES

It is evident that even before its release the Mint was concerned about the public confusing this coin with a quarter. This is indicated by several features distinct from the other silver coins of the day. The reverse design is a mirror image of that on the others, the word "LIBERTY" on the shield is in relief rather than incuse, and the edge is plain, not reeded. Nevertheless, the public was still confused, and the coin was terminated after only two years in circulation. The 1877 and 1878 dates are collectors' issues.

★ ★ COUNTERFEIT ALERT ★ ★

1876CC with added mintmark. Some 19th century charlatans would hand-scrape reeding into the edge of pieces in hopes of passing them off as quarters.

1876 Twenty-Cent Piece

	VG	VF
1875	240.00	375.00
1875CC	400.00	600.00
1875S	130.00	200.00
1876	250.00	385.00
1876CC, *extremely rare MS-65*		175,000.00
1877	—	3,100.00
1878	—	2,500.00

BUST QUARTERS

Due to limited mint capacity quarters were not struck until 1796, when a small quantity was produced, even though other denominations of United States silver were struck two years earlier. These first rare pieces were struck on blanks with crude edges, often exhibiting "adjustment marks" from filing off excess silver before striking. The initial reverse design, showing a rather skinny eagle within a wreath, had been in use only one year when the striking of quarters was suspended. When striking was resumed a few years later it was replaced with a plumper eagle carrying a heraldic shield. Coinage ceased again until 1815 when a cap was added to Liberty and her bust was turned to the left. In the same year a denomination first appeared, not as "quarter dollar," but as "25C."

Rare die combinations of early specimens command a premium from specialists. Cleaning plagues this series, and such pieces are discounted.

★ ★ COUNTERFEIT ALERT ★ ★

Cast counterfeits exist of 1796. Other counterfeits to 1807 are possible.

1796 Quarter with Draped Bust and Small Eagle

DRAPED BUST/SMALL EAGLE

	VG	VF
1796	16,500.00	36,500.00

1806 Quarter with Draped Bust and Heraldic Eagle

DRAPED BUST/HERALDIC EAGLE

	VG	VF		VG	VF
1804	4,200.00	8,600.00	1806	350.00	1,000.00
1805	360.00	1,000.00	1807	350.00	1,000.00
1806, 6 over 5	400.00	1,400.00			

1815 Quarter with Capped Bust

CAPPED BUST TYPE

	VG	VF		VG	VF
1815	120.00	410.00	1824, 4 over 2	400.00	1,500.00
1818, 8 over 5	120.00	450.00	1825, 5 over 2	180.00	520.00
1818	115.00	390.00	1825, 5 over 3	140.00	420.00
1819	115.00	390.00	1825, 5 over 4	125.00	400.00
1820	115.00	390.00	1827		70,000.00
1821	120.00	400.00	1827, proof restrike		75,000.00
1822, 25 over 50c	3,200.00	6,700.00	1828	110.00	375.00
1822	125.00	440.00	1828, 25 over 50c	300.00	1,200.00
1823, 3 over 2	30,000.00	56,000.00			

1833 Quarter with Capped Bust and No Motto (Reduced Size)

NO MOTTO, REDUCED SIZE

	VG	VF		VG	VF
1831, small letters	95.00	140.00	1835	90.00	150.00
1831, large letters	90.00	150.00	1836	90.00	150.00
1832	90.00	150.00	1837	90.00	150.00
1833	100.00	170.00	1838	90.00	150.00
1834	90.00	150.00			

SEATED LIBERTY QUARTERS

Following the introduction of the Seated Liberty design by Christian Gobrecht on the silver dollar, the smaller coins were gradually brought into harmony with this design. It is generally accepted that the seated goddess version of Liberty was directly or indirectly inspired by depictions of the Roman allegory of Britannia on British coins. The eagle on the reverse is not significantly different from that on the last capped bust coins.

There were several minor changes over the life of this coin. After the first few years, additional drapery was added below Liberty's elbow. The arrows by the date from 1853 to 1855, and the rays on the reverse in 1853 indicate a seven-percent reduction in weight, arrows in 1873 and 1874 saw a minuscule increase. A ribbon with the motto "In God We Trust" was added over the eagle in 1866.

★ ★ COUNTERFEIT ALERT ★ ★

Genuine 1858 quarters have been re-engraved to pass as 1853 no arrows pieces. Contemporary counterfeits struck in copper, lead, and white metal (tin and lead alloys) exist.

1847 Seated Liberty Quarter with No Motto Above Eagle

NO MOTTO ABOVE EAGLE

	VG	VF
1838	50.00	110.00
1839	44.00	100.00
1840O	55.00	135.00
1840, extra drapery from elbow	50.00	125.00
1840O, extra drapery from elbow	48.00	120.00

	VG	VF
1841	95.00	190.00
1841O	35.00	100.00
1842	125.00	285.00
1842O, small date	650.00	1,950.00
1842O, large date	45.00	75.00
1843	28.00	65.00
1843O	40.00	125.00
1844	27.00	65.00

1853O Seated Liberty Quarter with Arrows at Date and Rays on Reverse

	VG	VF
1844O	35.00	85.00
1845	27.00	65.00
1846	27.00	70.00
1847	27.00	68.00
1847O	45.00	140.00
1848	55.00	185.00
1849	30.00	65.00
1849O	700.00	1,850.00

	VG	VF
1850	55.00	135.00
1850O	50.00	120.00
1851	85.00	225.00
1851O	275.00	875.00
1852	80.00	195.00
1852O	270.00	900.00
1853, no arrows	550.00	1,050.00

1874S Seated Liberty Quarter with Arrows at Date

ARROWS AT DATE

	VG	VF
1853	27.00	55.00
1853, 3 over 4	75.00	250.00
1853O	42.00	100.00
1854	27.00	70.00
1854O	35.00	80.00

	VG	VF
1854O, huge O	1,400.00	4,800.00
1855	27.00	65.00
1855O	75.00	300.00
1855S	60.00	225.00

1856 Seated Liberty Quarter with Arrows Removed From Date

ARROWS REMOVED

	VG	VF
1856	27.00	45.00
1856O	35.00	65.00
1856S	70.00	350.00
1856S, S over S	200.00	975.00
1857	27.00	45.00
1857O	30.00	50.00
1857S	150.00	425.00
1858	27.00	45.00
1858O	35.00	70.00
1858S	110.00	300.00
1859	27.00	45.00
1859O	35.00	90.00

	VG	VF
1859S	175.00	500.00
1860	27.00	45.00
1860O	40.00	65.00
1860S	350.00	975.00
1861	27.00	45.00
1861S	135.00	450.00
1862	30.00	45.00
1862S	115.00	325.00
1863	47.00	130.00
1864	110.00	225.00
1864S	550.00	1,350.00
1865	110.00	225.00
1865S	150.00	400.00

1873 Seated Liberty Quarter, Open 3, with Motto Above Eagle

MOTTO ABOVE EAGLE

	VG	VF		VG	VF
1866	600.00	1,000.00	1871	60.00	135.00
1866S	365.00	1,050.00	1871CC	4,400.00	14,500.00
1867	325.00	685.00	1871S	465.00	1,100.00
1867S	425.00	925.00	1872	45.00	120.00
1868	225.00	400.00	1872CC	1,400.00	4,250.00
1868S	125.00	390.00	1872S	1,250.00	2,600.00
1869	475.00	800.00	1873, closed 3	325.00	725.00
1869S	135.00	385.00	1873, open 3	42.50	120.00
1870	85.00	225.00	1873CC		*four known*
1870CC	7,500.00	18,000.00			

ARROWS AT DATE

	VG	VF		VG	VF
1873	27.00	70.00	1874	27.00	70.00
1873CC	4,000.00	13,000.00	1874S	35.00	150.00
1873S	40.00	180.00			

1879 Seated Liberty Quarter with Arrows Removed From Date

ARROWS REMOVED

	VG	VF		VG	VF
1875	27.00	45.00	1880	235.00	335.00
1875CC	110.00	375.00	1881	235.00	375.00
1875S	56.00	120.00	1882	250.00	375.00
1876	27.00	45.00	1883	265.00	375.00
1876CC	50.00	75.00	1884	450.00	700.00
1876S	27.00	45.00	1885	265.00	375.00
1877	27.00	45.00	1886	600.00	825.00
1877CC	50.00	75.00	1887	375.00	575.00
1877S	27.00	45.00	1888	350.00	550.00
1877S, over horizontal S	60.00	175.00	1888S	30.00	45.00
			1889	300.00	425.00
1878	27.00	45.00	1890	90.00	150.00
1878CC	50.00	110.00	1891	30.00	45.00
1878S	185.00	350.00	1891O	235.00	575.00
1879	235.00	335.00	1891S	30.00	65.00

BARBER QUARTERS

The quarter, dime, and half dollar introduced in 1892 bear a portrait head of Liberty instead of an entire figure. They were designed by Chief Engraver Charles E. Barber, after whom they have been popularly named. More practical than artistically adventurous, contemporaries thought the design rather boring if not unpleasant. The reverse of the quarter and the half have a fully spread heraldic eagle, a ribbon in its beak, with a field of stars above. Barber quarters are very common and well worn examples are often regarded as little better than bullion.

★ ★ COUNTERFEIT ALERT ★ ★
Contemporary collectors counterfeits in a tin-lead alloy are not rare. 1913S suspected but not confirmed.

1896 Barber Quarter

	F	XF		F	XF
1892	25.00	75.00	1898O	75.00	300.00
1892O	42.00	96.00	1898S	50.00	100.00
1892S	80.00	190.00	1899	25.00	80.00
1893	28.00	75.00	1899O	35.00	135.00
1893O	30.00	100.00	1899S	75.00	145.00
1893S	63.00	165.00	1900	25.00	80.00
1894	34.00	95.00	1900O	65.00	160.00
1894O	42.00	125.00	1900S	40.00	85.00
1894S	38.00	120.00	1901	25.00	85.00
1895	35.00	85.00	1901O	135.00	470.00
1895O	40.00	135.00	1901S	16,500.00	28,000.00
1895S	60.00	150.00	1902	22.00	70.00
1896	25.00	85.00	1902O	52.00	160.00
1896O	115.00	425.00	1902S	55.00	175.00
1896S	1,850.00	4,350.00	1903	22.00	70.00
1897	25.00	80.00	1903O	42.00	125.00
1897O	115.00	400.00	1903S	50.00	145.00
1897S	275.00	440.00	1904	22.00	80.00
1898	25.00	80.00	1904O	63.00	250.00

1903 Barber Quarter

	F	XF
1905	30.00	80.00
1905O	85.00	260.00
1905S	45.00	125.00
1906	22.00	70.00
1906D	25.00	75.00
1906O	42.00	110.00
1907	22.00	66.00
1907D	30.00	85.00
1907O	22.00	70.00
1907S	50.00	175.00
1908	22.00	75.00
1908D	22.00	75.00
1908O	22.00	80.00
1908S	95.00	320.00
1909	22.00	70.00
1909D	25.00	90.00
1909O	95.00	395.00
1909S	38.00	100.00

	F	XF
1910	30.00	85.00
1910D	50.00	140.00
1911	22.00	80.00
1911D	100.00	350.00
1911S	55.00	175.00
1912	22.00	70.00
1912S	48.00	175.00
1913	75.00	415.00
1913D	40.00	98.00
1913S	3,950.00	6,500.00
1914	22.00	65.00
1914D	22.00	65.00
1914S	205.00	550.00
1915	22.00	66.00
1915D	22.00	66.00
1915S	37.00	120.00
1916	22.00	66.00
1916D	22.00	66.00

STANDING LIBERTY QUARTERS

According to many at the time, Hermon MacNeil's Standing Liberty quarter was America's first obscene coin. Many prominent artists thought it an excellent example of inspired neo-classical art. In either case, it was very well debated at the time. Its original version, with a bare-breasted Liberty stepping through a gateway while exposing a shield, was ultimately replaced by a more modest one on which she is clad in chain mail. The corrective legislation, however, was careful not to criticize the coin's artistic merit or moral standing openly, thus not offending the Commission of Fine Arts, responsible for its approval. Technically the coin shared with the Buffalo nickel the problem of a high relief date which would wear off. This was partially remedied in 1925 by carving out the area of the date and placing it in the recess. Another technical problem with this quarter was the tendency of Liberty's head to be incompletely struck. As a result high grade pieces with fully struck heads command extra premiums. Examples with the date worn off are worth only their bullion value.

★ ★ COUNTERFEIT ALERT ★ ★

1916 altered from 1917, 1917 Type I, 1918S 8 over 7, 1923S (altered, including all with round topped 3), 1927S (altered).

1916 Standing Liberty Quarter (Type I)

	F	XF		F	XF
1916	9,000.00	14,500.00	1918	30.00	55.00
1917	52.00	100.00	1918D	66.00	125.00
1917D	60.00	150.00	1918S	32.00	60.00
1917S	65.00	185.00	1918S, 8 over 7	3,850.00	8,250.00
1917	43.00	80.00	1919	55.00	85.00
1917D	65.00	125.00	1919D	195.00	600.00
1917S	63.00	125.00	1919S	185.00	540.00

	F	XF			F	XF
1920	25.00	55.00		1926S	12.00	110.00
1920D	88.00	175.00		1927	6.50	40.00
1920S	30.00	60.00		1927D	32.00	150.00
1921	450.00	800.00		1927S	110.00	1,200.00
1923	35.00	60.00		1928	6.50	40.00
1923S	675.00	1,300.00		1928D	8.00	45.00
1924	25.00	50.00		1928S	6.50	40.00
1924D	108.00	195.00		1929	6.50	40.00
1924S	43.00	110.00		1929D	7.00	45.00
1925	7.00	45.00		1929S	6.50	40.00
1926	6.50	40.00		1930	6.50	40.00
1926D	20.00	75.00		1930S	6.50	40.00

1927S Standing Liberty Quarter (Type II)

WASHINGTON QUARTERS

The Washington quarter was intended to be a one-year commemorative for the 200th anniversary of Washington's birth, not a regular issue. Its release was delayed because of the Treasury's decision to change designers from Laura Gardin Fraser to John Flanagan. Both designs were based on the 1785 bust of Washington by Houdon. Eventually it was decided to replace the unpopular Standing Liberty quarter with the new commemorative, which enjoyed immense initial popularity.

Several dates in the 1930s are characterized by weak rims making grading difficult. 1934 and 1935 do not have this problem. 1964 pieces were aggressively hoarded in uncirculated rolls, and as such are excessively common.

A special reverse was used in 1975 and 1976 (both with 1976 obverse) to commemorate the American Bicentennial. It depicts the bust of a Colonial drummer designed by Jack L. Ahr.

★ ★ COUNTERFEIT ALERT ★ ★

1932D and 1932S exist with false mintmarks. Counterfeits of high grade 1932 and 1934 pieces also exist.

1936D Washington Quarter

	VF	MS-65
1932	7.50	27.00
1932D	250.00	1,100.00
1932S	250.00	525.00
1934	5.20	30.00
1934D	14.00	245.00
1935	5.00	25.00
1935D	14.00	255.00

	VF	MS-65
1935S	7.50	110.00
1936	5.00	25.00
1936D	22.00	625.00
1936S	6.25	150.00
1937	5.00	26.00
1937D	6.25	70.00
1937S	15.00	160.00

1945 Washington Quarter

	VF	MS-65		VF	MS-65
1938	7.00	90.00	1944	—	6.50
1938S	10.00	110.00	1944D	5.00	20.00
1939	5.00	16.00	1944S	5.00	16.00
1939D	5.50	45.00	1945	—	6.00
1939S	9.00	110.00	1945D	5.00	19.00
1940	4.50	20.00	1945S	—	10.00
1940D	12.50	135.00	1946	—	6.00
1940S	6.50	28.00	1946D	—	9.50
1941	—	10.00	1946S	—	9.00
1941D	—	35.00	1947	—	11.00
1941S	—	31.00	1947D	—	9.50
1942	—	8.00	1947S	—	9.50
1942D	—	19.00	1948	—	6.00
1942S	5.00	80.00	1948D	—	12.00
1943	—	6.50	1948S	—	8.00
1943D	5.00	30.00	1949	6.50	38.00
1943S	5.00	30.00	1949D	—	18.00

1953D Washington Quarter (Silver)

1966 Washington Quarter (Cupro-Nickel Clad Copper)

	VF	MS-65		VF	MS-65
1950	—	6.50	1955D	5.00	6.00
1950D	—	6.50	1956	—	6.00
1950D, D over S	65.00	295.00	1956D	—	5.50
1950S	—	9.50	1957	—	6.00
1950S, S over D	70.00	400.00	1957D	—	6.00
1951	—	6.00	1958	—	5.75
1951D	—	7.00	1958D	—	5.25
1951S	—	23.00	1959	—	5.00
1952	—	6.50	1959D	—	5.00
1952D	—	5.50	1960	—	5.00
1952S	5.00	20.00	1960D	—	5.00
1953	—	5.50	1961	—	5.00
1953D	—	5.50	1961D	—	5.00
1953S	—	5.50	1962	—	5.00
1954	—	6.00	1962D	—	5.00
1954D	—	6.00	1963	—	5.00
1954S	—	5.50	1963D	—	5.00
1955	—	5.50	1964	—	5.00
			1964D	—	5.00

1976 Washington Quarter with Bicentennial Reverse

CUPRO-NICKEL CLAD COPPER

	MS-65
1965	—......1.00
1966	—......1.00
1967	—......1.00
1968	—......1.00
1968D	—......1.25
1968S, *proof only*	—......3.50
1969	—......1.25
1969D	—......1.00
1969S, *proof only*	—......3.50
1970	—......1.00
1970D	—......1.00
1970S, *proof only*	—......3.00
1971	—......1.00
1971D	—......1.00
1971S, *proof only*	—......3.00
1972	—......75
1972D	—......75
1972S, *proof only*	—......3.00
1973	—......75
1973D	—......1.00
1973S, *proof only*	—......3.00
1974	—......75
1974D	—......1.00
1974S, *proof only*	—......3.00
1976, Bicentennial	—......1.00
1976D, Bicentennial	—......1.00
1976S, Bicentennial, *proof only*	—......2.00
1976S, Bicentennial, Silver Clad	—......3.00
1977	—......75
1977D	—......75
1977S, *proof only*	—......2.00
1978	—......75
1978D	—......75

	MS-65
1978S, *proof only*	—......2.00
1979	—......75
1979D	—......75
1979, thick S, *proof only*	—......2.00
1979, thin S, *proof only*	—......3.00
1980P	—......75
1980D	—......75
1980S, *proof only*	—......2.00

	MS-65
1981P	—......75
1981D	—......75
1981S, *proof only*	—......2.00
1982P	—......3.00
1982D	—......1.50
1982S, *proof only*	—......3.00
1983P	—......3.00
1983D	—......2.00
1983S, *proof only*	—......2.75
1984P	—......1.00
1984D	—......1.25
1984S, *proof only*	—......2.75
1985P	—......1.50
1985D	—......2.00
1985S, *proof only*	—......1.75
1986P	—......3.00
1986D	—......2.00
1986S, *proof only*	—......3.00
1987P	—......75
1987D	—......75
1987S, *proof only*	—......2.00
1988P	—......1.00
1988D	—......1.00
1988S, *proof only*	—......2.25
1989P	—......75
1989D	—......75
1989S, *proof only*	—......2.25
1990P	—......75
1990D	—......75
1990S, *proof only*	—......6.00
1991P	—......75
1991D	—......75
1991S, *proof only*	—......3.00
1992P	—......75
1992D	—......75
1992S, *proof only*	—......3.25
1992S, Silver, *proof only*	—......4.00
1993P	—......75
1993D	—......75
1993S, *proof only*	—......3.00
1993S, Silver, *proof only*	—......6.50
1994P	—......75
1994D	—......75
1994S, *proof only*	—......4.00
1994S, Silver, *proof only*	—.....12.50
1995P	—......75

	MS-65
1995D. . . . .—. 75	
1995S, *proof only* . . . .—. 18.00	
1995S, Silver, *proof only* . .—. 18.00	
1996P. . . . .—. 75	
1996D. . . . .—. 75	
1996S, *proof only* . . . .—. 4.50	
1996S, Silver, *proof only* . .—. 12.50	
1997P. . . . .—. 75	
1997D. . . . .—. 75	

	MS-65
1997S, *proof only* . . . .—. 11.00	
1997S, Silver,	
proof only . . . .—. . . . 22.00	
1998P. . . . .—. 75	
1998D . . . .—. 75	
1998S, *proof only* . . . .—. 11.00	
1998S, Silver,	
proof only . . . .—. . . . 12.50	

STATE QUARTERS

In 1992, to commemorate its 125th anniversary, Canada released a set of circulating commemorative quarters honoring each province and territory. They were greeted with immense popularity by the general public. Partially inspired by this Canadian series, the United States issued a similar set of quarters honoring the 50 states. It was the intent of Congress to "promote the diffusion of knowledge among the youth of the United States about the individual states, their history and geography, and the rich diversity of the national heritage."

Five each year were released from 1999 to 2008. Their release dates were in the order by which each state ratified the Constitution, with a new quarter appearing roughly every 10 weeks. These were the only quarters issued during these years. None with the eagle reverse were produced at all.

The designs had to meet certain federal criteria, but were designed and submitted at a state level. Many were provided by public competitions.

In addition to clad circulation strikes, special silver and clad proof coins were produced for collectors, much as they have been in previous years.

★ COUNTERFEIT ★ ALERT

Apparently risqué designs are actually satirical tokens struck with privately made dies on real quarters.

State Quarter Front

Delaware (1999)

Pennsylvania (1999)

	MS-65	PRF-65
1999P Delaware	—	1.50
1999D Delaware	—	1.50
1999S Delaware, *proof only*	—	15.00
1999S Delaware, Silver, *proof only*	—	65.00

	MS-65	PRF-65
1999P Pennsylvania	—	1.50
1999D Pennsylvania	—	1.50
1999S Pennsylvania, *proof only*	—	15.00
1999S Pennsylvania, Silver, *proof only*	—	65.00

New Jersey (1999)

Georgia (1999)

	MS-65	PRF-65
1999P New Jersey	—	1.50
1999D New Jersey	—	1.50
1999S New Jersey, *proof only*	—	15.00
1999S New Jersey, Silver, *proof only*	—	65.00

	MS-65	PRF-65
1999P Georgia	—	1.50
1999D Georgia	—	1.50
1999S Georgia, *proof only*	—	15.00
1999S Georgia, Silver, *proof only*	—	65.00

Connecticut (1999)

Massachusetts (2000)

	MS-65	PRF-65
1999P Connecticut	—	.75
1999D Connecticut	—	.75
1999S Connecticut, *proof only*	—	15.00
1999S Connecticut, Silver, *proof only*	—	65.00

	MS-65	PRF-65
2000P Massachusetts	—	.75
2000D Massachusetts	—	.75
2000S Massachusetts, *proof only*	—	5.00
2000S Massachusetts, Silver, *proof only*	—	10.00

Maryland (2000)

South Carolina (2000)

	MS-65	PRF-65
2000P Maryland	—	.75
2000D Maryland	—	.75
2000S Maryland, *proof only*	—	5.00
2000S Maryland, Silver, *proof only*	—	10.00

	MS-65	PRF-65
2000P South Carolina	—	.75
2000D South Carolina	—	.75
2000S South Carolina, *proof only*	—	5.00
2000S South Carolina, Silver, *proof only*	—	10.00

New Hampshire (2000)

Virginia (2000)

	MS-65	PRF-65
2000P New Hampshire	—	.75
2000D New Hampshire	—	.75
2000S New Hampshire, proof only	—	5.00
2000S New Hampshire, Silver, proof only	—	10.00

	MS-65	PRF-65
2000P Virginia	—	.75
2000D Virginia	—	.75
2000S Virginia, proof only	—	5.00
2000S Virginia, Silver, proof only	—	10.00

New York (2001)

North Carolina (2001)

	MS-65	PRF-65
2001P New York	—	.75
2001D New York	—	.75
2001S New York, proof only	—	9.50
2001S New York, Silver, proof only	—	22.50

	MS-65	PRF-65
2001P North Carolina	—	.75
2001D North Carolina	—	.75
2001S North Carolina, proof only	—	9.50
2001S North Carolina, Silver, proof only	—	22.50

Rhode Island (2001)

Vermont (2001)

	MS-65	PRF-65
2001P Rhode Island	—	.75
2001D Rhode Island	—	.75
2001S Rhode Island, proof only	—	9.50
2001S Rhode Island, Silver, proof only	—	22.50

	MS-65	PRF-65
2001P Vermont	—	1.00
2001D Vermont	—	.75
2001S Vermont, proof only	—	9.50
2001S Vermont, Silver, proof only	—	22.50

Kentucky (2001)

Tennessee (2002)

	MS-65	PRF-65
2001P Kentucky	—	1.00
2001D Kentucky	—	.75
2001S Kentucky, proof only	—	9.50
2001S Kentucky, Silver, proof only	—	22.50

	MS-65	PRF-65
2002P Tennessee	—	1.75
2002D Tennessee	—	1.75
2002S Tennessee, proof only	—	6.00
2002S Tennessee, Silver, proof only	—	11.00

Ohio (2002)

Louisiana (2002)

	MS-65	PRF-65
2002P Ohio	—	.75
2002D Ohio	—	.75
2002S Ohio, *proof only*	—	6.00
2002S Ohio, Silver, *proof only*	—	11.00

	MS-65	PRF-65
2002P Louisiana	—	.75
2002D Louisiana	—	.75
2002S Louisiana, *proof only*	—	6.00
2002S Louisiana, Silver, *proof only*	—	11.00

Indiana (2002)

Mississippi (2002)

	MS-65	PRF-65
2002P Indiana	—	.75
2002D Indiana	—	.75
2002S Indiana, *proof only*	—	6.00
2002S Indiana, Silver, *proof only*	—	11.00

	MS-65	PRF-65
2002P Mississippi	—	.75
2002D Mississippi	—	.75
2002S Mississippi, *proof only*	—	6.00
2002S Mississippi, Silver, *proof only*	—	11.00

Illinois (2003)

Alabama (2003)

	MS-65	PRF-65
2003P Illinois	—	.75
2003D Illinois	—	.75
2003S Illinois, proof only	—	4.00
2003S Illinois, Silver, proof only	—	6.00

	MS-65	PRF-65
2003P Alabama	—	.75
2003D Alabama	—	.75
2003S Alabama, proof only	—	4.00
2003S Alabama, Silver, proof only	—	6.00

Maine (2003)

Missouri (2003)

	MS-65	PRF-65
2003P Maine	—	.75
2003D Maine	—	.75
2003S Maine, proof only	—	4.00
2003S Maine, Silver, proof only	—	6.00

	MS-65	PRF-65
2003P Missouri	—	.75
2003D Missouri	—	.75
2003S Missouri, proof only	—	4.00
2003S Missouri, Silver, proof only	—	6.00

Arkansas (2003)

Michigan (2004)

	MS-65	PRF-65
2003P Arkansas	—	.75
2003D Arkansas	—	.75
2003S Arkansas, proof only	—	4.00
2003S Arkansas, Silver, proof only	—	6.00

	MS-65	PRF-65
2004P Michigan	—	.75
2004D Michigan	—	.75
2004S Michigan, proof only	—	4.00
2004S Michigan, Silver, proof only	—	6.00

Florida (2004)

Texas (2004)

	MS-65	PRF-65
2004P Florida	—	.75
2004D Florida	—	.75
2004S Florida, proof only	—	6.00
2004S Florida, Silver, proof only	—	10.00

	MS-65	PRF-65
2004P Texas	—	.75
2004D Texas	—	.75
2004S Texas, proof only	—	5.00
2004S Texas, Silver, proof only	—	6.00

Iowa (2004)

Wisconsin (2004)

	MS-65	PRF-65
2004P Iowa	—	.75
2004D Iowa	—	.75
2004S Iowa,		
proof only	—	5.00
2004S Iowa, Silver,		
proof only	—	6.00

	MS-65	PRF-65
2004P Wisconsin	—	.75
2004D Wisconsin	—	.75
2004S Wisconsin,		
proof only	—	5.00
2004S Wisconsin, Silver,		
proof only	—	6.00

California (2005)

Minnesota (2005)

	MS-65	PRF-65
2005P California	—	1.00
2005D California	—	1.00
2005S California,		
proof only	—	3.00
2005S California, Silver,		
proof only	—	6.00

	MS-65	PRF-65
2005P Minnesota	—	1.00
2005D Minnesota	—	1.00
2005S Minnesota,		
proof only	—	3.00
2005S Minnesota, Silver,		
proof only	—	6.00

Oregon (2005)

Kansas (2005)

	MS-65	PRF-65
2005P Oregon	—	1.00
2005D Oregon	—	1.00
2005S Oregon, proof only	—	3.00
2005S Oregon, Silver, proof only	—	6.00

	MS-65	PRF-65
2005P Kansas	—	1.00
2005D Kansas	—	1.00
2005S Kansas, proof only	—	3.00
2005S Kansas, Silver, proof only	—	6.00

West Virginia (2005)

	MS-65	PRF-65
2005P West Virginia	—	1.00
2005D West Virginia	—	1.00
2005S West Virginia, proof only	—	3.00
2005S West Virginia, Silver, proof only	—	6.00

Nevada (2006)

Nebraska (2006)

	MS-65	PRF-65
2006P Nevada	—	1.00
2006D Nevada	—	1.00
2006S Nevada, proof only	—	4.00
2006S Nevada, Silver, proof only	—	6.00

	MS-65	PRF-65
2006P Nebraska	—	1.00
2006D Nebraska	—	1.00
2006S Nebraska, proof only	—	4.00
2006S Nebraska, Silver, proof only	—	6.00

Colorado (2006)

North Dakota (2006)

	MS-65	PRF-65
2006P Colorado	—	1.00
2006D Colorado	—	1.00
2006S Colorado, proof only	—	4.00
2006S Colorado, Silver, proof only	—	6.00

	MS-65	PRF-65
2006P North Dakota	—	1.00
2006D North Dakota	—	1.00
2006S North Dakota, proof only	—	4.00
2006S North Dakota, Silver, proof only	—	6.00

South Dakota (2006)

Montana (2007)

	MS-65	PRF-65
2006P South Dakota	—	1.00
2006D South Dakota	—	1.00
2006S South Dakota, *proof only*	—	4.00
2006S South Dakota, Silver, *proof only*	—	6.00

	MS-65	PRF-65
2007P Montana	—	1.00
2007D Montana	—	1.00
2007S Montana, *proof only*	—	4.00
2007S Montana, Silver, *proof only*	—	6.00

Washington (2007)

Idaho (2007)

	MS-65	PRF-65
2007P Washington	—	1.00
2007D Washington	—	1.00
2007S Washington, *proof only*	—	4.00
2007S Washington, Silver, *proof only*	—	6.00

	MS-65	PRF-65
2007P Idaho	—	1.00
2007D Idaho	—	1.00
2007S Idaho, *proof only*	—	4.00
2007S Idaho, Silver, *proof only*	—	6.00

Wyoming (2007)

Utah (2007)

	MS-65	PRF-65
2007P Wyoming	—	1.00
2007D Wyoming	—	1.00
2007S Wyoming, *proof only*	—	4.00
2007S Wyoming, Silver, *proof only*	—	6.00

	MS-65	PRF-65
2007P Utah	—	1.00
2007D Utah	—	1.00
2007S Utah, *proof only*	—	4.50
2007S Utah, Silver, *proof only*	—	6.50

Oklahoma (2008)

New Mexico (2008)

	MS-65	PRF-65
2008P Oklahoma	—	1.00
2008D Oklahoma	—	1.00
2008S Oklahoma, *proof only*	—	4.50
2008S Oklahoma, Silver, *proof only*	—	6.50

	MS-65	PRF-65
2008P New Mexico	—	1.00
2008D New Mexico	—	1.00
2008S New Mexico, *proof only*	—	4.50
2008S New Mexico, Silver, *proof only*	—	6.50

Arizona (2008)

Alaska (2008)

	MS-65	PRF-65
2008P Arizona	—	1.00
2008D Arizona	—	1.00
2008S Arizona, proof only	—	4.50
2008S Arizona, Silver, proof only	—	6.50

	MS-65	PRF-65
2008P Alaska	—	1.00
2008D Alaska	—	1.00
2008S Alaska, proof only	—	4.50
2008S Alaska, Silver, proof only	—	6.50

Hawaii (2008)

	MS-65	PRF-65
2008P Hawaii	—	1.00
2008D Hawaii	—	1.00
2008S Hawaii, proof only	—	4.50
2008S Hawaii, Silver, proof only	—	6.50

EARLY HALF DOLLARS

The half dollar, along with the half dime and dollar, was one of the first silver denominations to be released by the new United States Mint. As a result, it first appeared with the briefly used flowing hair design. These first rare pieces were struck on blanks with crude edges and often exhibit "adjustment marks" from filing off excess silver before striking. The initial reverse design showing a rather skinny eagle within a wreath continued to be used after the flowing hair obverse was replaced by the rather voluptuous draped bust design. After a brief gap in the issue of halves, this eagle was replaced with a plumper eagle carrying a heraldic shield. In 1807, a cap was added to Liberty's head and her bust was turned to the left. That same year a denomination first appeared, not as "half dollar," but as "50C." The eagle was also made slightly more realistic, though it still bore a heraldic shield. With the introduction of this type, production increased. By the 1910s and 1920s, halves became so common that banks used them as cash reserves to back up their own privately issued paper money. As a result, many half dollars between 1807 and 1839 can be found very well preserved. Unfortunately their high relief caused many of them to be incompletely struck, particularly at the motto over the eagle, and the broach. In 1836 new machinery was introduced, and the edges were changed from lettered to reeded.

Rare die combinations of early specimens command a premium from specialists. Cleaning plagues this series, and such pieces are discounted.

★ ★ COUNTERFEIT ALERT ★ ★

Cast counterfeits exist of 1796. Other counterfeits of 1794 to 1802 are possible. Contemporary counterfeits of capped bust halves exist for most dates. They have been struck or cast in brass, copper, tin-lead alloys, and German silver. Holed coins are sometimes deceptively plugged.

1795 Half Dollar with Flowing Hair

FLOWING HAIR TYPE

	VG	VF
1794	6,500.00	19,500.00
1795, two leaves	1,500.00	4,000.00

	VG	VF
1795, three leaves	3,000.00	9,900.00

1797 Half Dollar with Draped Bust and Small Eagle

DRAPED BUST/SMALL EAGLE

	VG	VF
1796, 15 stars	39,500.00	87,000.00
1796, 16 stars	48,000.00	90,000.00

	VG	VF
1797	39,500.00	87,000.00

1807 Half Dollar with Draped Bust and Heraldic Eagle

DRAPED BUST/HERALDIC EAGLE

	VG	VF
1801	1,200.00	3,950.00
1802	1,100.00	3,900.00
1803, small 3	270.00	1,100.00
1803, large 3	240.00	900.00
1805, 5 over 4	325.00	1,200.00

	VG	VF
1805	240.00	550.00
1806, 6 over 5	240.00	525.00
1806	240.00	525.00
Note: many varieties of 1806 exist.		
1807	240.00	525.00

1836 Half Dollar with Capped Bust and Lettered Edge

CAPPED BUST/LETTERED EDGE

	VG	VF
1807, small stars	175.00	550.00
1807, large stars	165.00	475.00
1807, 50 over 20	125.00	350.00
1808, 8 over 7	110.00	250.00
1808	85.00	140.00
1809	85.00	140.00
1810	85.00	140.00
1811, 11 over 10	95.00	155.00
1811	85.00	125.00
1812, 2 over 1, small 8	90.00	195.00
1812, 2 over 1, large 8	1,900.00	4,800.00
1812	83.00	130.00
1813	83.00	130.00
1813, 50 C over inverted UNI	95.00	185.00
1814, 4 over 3	135.00	290.00
1814	83.00	130.00
1815, 5 over 2	1,500.00	2,900.00
1817, 7 over 3	185.00	515.00
1817, 7 over 4	80,000.00	200,000.00
1817	83.00	130.00
1818, 8 over 7	100.00	140.00
1818	80.00	115.00
1819, 9 over 8	80.00	120.00
1819	80.00	115.00
1820, 20 over 19	110.00	200.00
1820	80.00	145.00
1821	80.00	115.00
1822, 2 over 1	90.00	190.00
1822	80.00	115.00
1823	80.00	110.00
1824, 4 over 1	80.00	115.00
1824, 4 over 4	80.00	115.00
1824	80.00	115.00
1825	80.00	115.00
1826	80.00	115.00
1827, 7 over 6	100.00	160.00
1827	80.00	115.00
1828	80.00	115.00
Note: date varieties of 1828 exist.		
1829, 9 over 7	85.00	175.00
1829	75.00	90.00
1830	70.00	90.00
1831	70.00	90.00
1832	70.00	90.00
1833	70.00	90.00
1834	70.00	90.00
1835	70.00	90.00
1836	70.00	90.00
1836, 50 over 00	100.00	195.00

1836 Half Dollar with Capped Bust and Reeded Edge

CAPPED BUST/REEDED EDGE

	VG	VF		VG	VF
1836, 50 cents	1,200.00	2,100.00	1838O, *proof only*		300,000.00
1837, 50 cents	75.00	125.00	1839, half dol.	75.00	150.00
1838, half dol.	75.00	125.00	1839O, half dol.	320.00	675.00

SEATED LIBERTY HALF DOLLARS

Following the introduction of the Seated Liberty design by Christian Gobrecht on the silver dollar, the smaller coins were gradually brought into harmony with this design. The half dollar was the last to make the change. It is generally accepted that the seated goddess version of Liberty was directly or indirectly inspired by depictions of the Roman allegory of Britannia on British coins. The eagle on the reverse is not significantly different from that on the last capped bust coins.

There were several minor changes over the life of this coin. During its first year additional drapery was added below Liberty's elbow. The arrows by the date from 1853 to 1855, and the rays on the reverse in 1853 indicate a seven-percent reduction in weight, arrows in 1873 and 1874 saw a minuscule increase. Most of the 1861O pieces were struck after Louisiana seceded from the Union. A ribbon with the motto "In God We Trust" was added over the eagle in 1866. Seated halves are often found cleaned. Be careful of retoned specimens.

★ ★ COUNTERFEIT ALERT ★ ★

Genuine 1858O halves have been re-engraved to pass as 1853O no arrows pieces. Some with arrows pieces have had the arrows removed for the same reason. Contemporary counterfeits struck in tin and lead alloys are often found.

1839 Seated Liberty Half Dollar with No Motto
Above Eagle and No Drapery Below Elbow

NO MOTTO ABOVE EAGLE

	VG	VF
1839, no drapery below elbow	85.00	340.00
1839, with drapery	45.00	88.00
1840, sm. rev. letters	45.00	85.00
1840, med. rev. letters (struck at New Orleans with 1838 reverse die)	175.00	325.00
1840O	45.00	90.00
1841	65.00	150.00
1841O	40.00	90.00
1842, small date	50.00	110.00
1842, large date	45.00	90.00
1842O, small date	850.00	2,350.00
1842O, large date	40.00	90.00
1843	40.00	70.00
1843O	40.00	70.00
1844	40.00	70.00
1844O	40.00	70.00
1844O, double date	775.00	1,375.00
1845	40.00	110.00
1845O	40.00	70.00
1845O, no drapery	47.00	115.00
1846	40.00	70.00
1846, 6 over horizontal 6	250.00	435.00
1846O, med. date	40.00	70.00
1846O, tall date	285.00	620.00
1847, 7 over 6	2,700.00	5,200.00
1847	45.00	70.00
1847O	40.00	70.00
1848	65.00	190.00
1848O	40.00	70.00
1849	45.00	80.00
1849O	40.00	70.00
1850	320.00	560.00
1850O	40.00	80.00
1851	425.00	800.00
1851O	55.00	120.00
1852	500.00	925.00
1852O	125.00	350.00
1853O, no arrows	154,000.00	rare

1853 Seated Liberty Half Dollar with Arrows at Date and Rays on Reverse

ARROWS AT DATE/
RAYS ON REVERSE

	VG	VF		VG	VF
1853	35.00	98.00	1853O	35.00	135.00

1854 Seated Liberty Half Dollar with Arrows at Date, No Rays on Reverse

ARROWS AT DATE/NO RAYS

	VG	VF		VG	VF
1854	38.00	70.00	1855	40.00	75.00
1854O	38.00	70.00	1855O	38.00	70.00
1855, over 1854	85.00	275.00	1855S	500.00	1,500.00

1858S Seated Liberty Half Dollar with Arrows Removed From Date

ARROWS REMOVED

	VG	VF		VG	VF
1856	38.00	70.00	1860S	38.00	75.00
1856O	38.00	70.00	1861	38.00	70.00
1856S	98.00	280.00	1861O	38.00	70.00
1857	38.00	70.00	1861S	40.00	70.00
1857O	38.00	70.00	1862	50.00	130.00
1857S	115.00	290.00	1862S	38.00	70.00
1858	38.00	70.00	1863	45.00	80.00
1858O	38.00	70.00	1863S	40.00	70.00
1858S	45.00	115.00	1864	45.00	110.00
1859	38.00	70.00	1864S	38.00	70.00
1859O	38.00	70.00	1865	45.00	90.00
1859S	40.00	115.00	1865S	38.00	70.00
1860	40.00	90.00	1866	—	unique
1860O	38.00	70.00	1866S	325.00	800.00

1872CC Seated Liberty Half Dollar with Motto Above Eagle

MOTTO ABOVE EAGLE

	VG	VF
1866	40.00	75.00
1866S	38.00	70.00
1867	48.00	120.00
1867S	40.00	70.00
1868	60.00	190.00
1868S	40.00	70.00
1869	40.00	70.00
1869S	42.00	70.00
1870	40.00	75.00
1870CC	1,600.00	5,500.00
1870S	40.00	75.00
1871	40.00	70.00
1871CC	325.00	1,200.00
1871S	40.00	70.00
1872	40.00	70.00
1872CC	125.00	450.00
1872S	45.00	135.00
1873, closed 3	45.00	120.00
1873, open 3	3,500.00	5,900.00
1873CC	320.00	900.00
1873S *No known specimens.*		

1873 Seated Liberty Half Dollar with Arrows at Date

ARROWS AT DATE

	VG	VF
1873	50.00	110.00
1873CC	275.00	925.00
1873S	80.00	265.00
1874	45.00	110.00
1874CC	575.00	1,800.00
1874S	60.00	220.00

1878S Seated Liberty Half Dollar with Arrows Removed From Date

ARROWS REMOVED

	VG	VF		VG	VF
1875	38.00	70.00	1880	325.00	450.00
1875CC	56.00	120.00	1881	300.00	400.00
1875S	38.00	70.00	1882	400.00	500.00
1876	38.00	70.00	1883	350.00	460.00
1876CC	55.00	115.00	1884	420.00	550.00
1876S	38.00	70.00	1885	400.00	550.00
1877	38.00	70.00	1886	500.00	725.00
1877CC	55.00	115.00	1887	600.00	800.00
1877S	38.00	70.00	1888	325.00	425.00
1878	45.00	90.00	1889	325.00	425.00
1878CC	600.00	1,550.00	1890	325.00	425.00
1878S	35,000.00	44,000.00	1891	65.00	130.00
1879	325.00	450.00			

BARBER HALF DOLLARS

The half dollar, quarter, and dime introduced in 1892 bear a portrait of Liberty's head, instead of an entire figure. They were designed by Chief Engraver Charles E. Barber, after whom they have been popularly named. Rather practical than artistically adventurous, contemporaries thought the design rather boring, if not unpleasant. The reverse of the half and the quarter have a fully spread heraldic eagle, a ribbon in its beak, with a field of stars above. This new design for the half dollar came only a year following its resurrection as an actively minted denomination. Barbers are very common, and well-worn examples are often regarded as little better than bullion. Strong middle grades on the other hand are surprisingly difficult to obtain.

★ ★ COUNTERFEIT ALERT ★ ★

Contemporary counterfeits in a tin-lead alloy are not rare. Altered 1913, 1914, and 1915 coins exist with mintmarks removed.

1892 Barber Half Dollar

	VG	VF		VG	VF
1892	42.00	125.00	1895O	38.00	230.00
1892O	400.00	590.00	1895S	55.00	250.00
1892S	325.00	550.00	1896	28.00	155.00
1893	30.00	135.00	1896O	55.00	300.00
1893O	60.00	225.00	1896S	135.00	350.00
1893S	225.00	550.00	1897	15.00	100.00
1894	50.00	200.00	1897O	230.00	850.00
1894O	31.00	175.00	1897S	200.00	550.00
1894S	28.00	125.00	1898	15.00	96.00
1895	25.00	150.00	1898O	75.00	355.00

1903 Barber Half Dollar

1908O Barber Half Dollar

	VG	VF
1898S	50.00	175.00
1899	15.00	100.00
1899O	36.00	175.00
1899S	33.00	150.00
1900	16.00	96.00
1900O	23.00	175.00
1900S	19.00	100.00
1901	16.00	96.00
1901O	28.00	205.00
1901S	55.00	355.00
1902	14.00	90.00
1902O	17.00	110.00
1902S	19.00	150.00
1903	16.00	125.00
1903O	17.00	125.00
1903S	18.00	125.00
1904	14.00	90.00
1904O	33.00	225.00
1904S	70.00	550.00
1905	28.00	180.00
1905O	50.00	250.00
1905S	17.00	125.00
1906	15.00	90.00
1906D	14.00	100.00
1906O	14.00	110.00
1906S	16.00	120.00
1907	14.00	90.00
1907D	14.00	85.00

	VG	VF
1907O	14.00	100.00
1907S	22.00	175.00
1908	14.00	90.00
1908D	14.00	90.00
1908O	14.00	100.00
1908S	25.00	175.00
1909	16.00	100.00
1909O	23.00	140.00
1909S	14.00	100.00
1910	29.00	175.00
1910S	17.00	100.00
1911	14.00	90.00
1911D	16.00	100.00
1911S	17.00	100.00
1912	14.00	90.00
1912D	14.00	90.00
1912S	20.00	100.00
1913	75.00	420.00
1913D	20.00	100.00
1913S	25.00	120.00
1914	170.00	550.00
1914S	19.00	100.00
1915	165.00	380.00
1915D	14.00	85.00
1915S	20.00	100.00

WALKING LIBERTY HALF DOLLARS

This artistic new half dollar was designed by Adolph Weinman, the designer of the Mercury dime released in the same year. It depicts Liberty, the American flag draped about her and flowing in the breeze, progressing towards the dawn of a new day. It was received with wide acclaim for its artistic merit when it was first released as part of a program for the beautification of United States coinage. The reverse carries an eagle perched on a rocky crag. The obverse design proved so popular that it was resurrected in 1986 for use on the new silver one-ounce bullion coins. Originally the mintmarks on this coin appeared on the obverse, but after a matter of months they were moved to the reverse.

Due to the arrangement of the design, Liberty's head does not always strike up fully. High grade examples with fully struck heads are worth more.

★ ★ COUNTERFEIT ALERT ★ ★

1916S, 1938D coins with added mintmark exist. 1928D halves are all counterfeit.

1921D Walking Liberty Half Dollar

	F	XF		F	XF
1916	110.00	275.00	1917S, rev.	18.00	70.00
1916D	90.00	250.00	1918	18.00	170.00
1916S	300.00	700.00	1918D	38.00	250.00
1917	11.00	50.00	1918S	17.00	70.00
1917D, obv.	90.00	240.00	1919	85.00	575.00
1917D, rev.	50.00	300.00	1919D	110.00	850.00
1917S, obv.	150.00	750.00	1919S	85.00	990.00

1944 Walking Liberty Half Dollar

	F	XF		F	XF
1920	18.00	80.00	1939	—	10.00
1920D	75.00	500.00	1939D	—	10.00
1920S	22.00	260.00	1939S	—	14.00
1921	375.00	1,750.00	1940	—	10.00
1921D	600.00	2,300.00	1940S	—	11.00
1921S	250.00	5,200.00	1941	—	10.00
1923S	30.00	350.00	1941D	—	10.00
1927S	15.00	185.00	1941S	—	10.00
1928S	16.50	210.00	1942	—	10.00
1929D	19.00	115.00	1942D	—	10.00
1929S	13.50	125.00	1942D, D over S	45.00	85.00
1933S	13.50	68.00	1942S	—	10.00
1934	10.00	14.00	1943	—	10.00
1934D	10.00	35.00	1943D	—	10.00
1934S	10.00	30.00	1943S	—	10.00
1935	—	10.00	1944	—	10.00
1935D	—	31.00	1944D	—	10.00
1935S	—	29.00	1944S	—	10.00
1936	—	10.00	1945	—	10.00
1936D	—	20.00	1945D	—	10.00
1936S	—	22.00	1945S	—	10.00
1937	—	10.00	1946	—	10.00
1937D	—	34.00	1946D	—	23.00
1937S	—	25.00	1946S	—	10.00
1938	—	11.00	1947	—	10.00
1938D	180.00	240.00	1947D	—	12.50

FRANKLIN HALF DOLLARS

Like the design for the Washington quarter, the design for the Franklin half dollar was used in opposition to the recommendation of the Commission of Fine Arts. The reverse depicts the Liberty Bell as its prime motif, despite a law requiring all coins larger than a dime to bear an eagle. This is why a small eagle was added at the side of the bell as an afterthought. While the coin was designed by Chief Engraver John R. Sinnock, the minute eagle was actually engraved by a young Frank Gasparro.

The biggest striking problem of the Franklin half dollar is the horizontal lines on the Liberty Bell. Those mint-state examples with fully struck bell lines often sell for significantly more.

★ ★ COUNTERFEIT ALERT ★ ★

It is possible that none exist.

1953 Franklin Half Dollar

	XF	MS-60		XF	MS-60
1948	10.00	17.00	1952	—	12.00
1948D	10.00	17.00	1952D	—	12.00
1949	10.00	40.00	1952S	21.00	50.00
1949D	15.00	45.00	1953	11.00	25.00
1949S	20.00	65.00	1953D	—	12.00
1950	10.00	27.00	1953S	—	26.00
1950D	10.00	23.00	1954	—	12.00
1951	—	12.00	1954D	—	12.00
1951D	14.00	28.00	1954S	—	15.00
1951S	12.00	24.00	1955	19.00	30.00

1962 Franklin Half Dollar

	XF	MS-60		XF	MS-60
1955, "Bugs Bunny"			1959D	—	12.00
teeth	—	28.00	1960	—	12.00
1956	10.00	13.00	1960D	—	12.00
1957	—	12.00	1961	—	12.00
1957D	—	12.00	1961D	—	12.00
1958	—	12.00	1962	—	12.00
1958D	—	12.00	1962D	—	12.00
1959	—	12.00	1963	—	12.00
			1963D	—	12.00

KENNEDY HALF DOLLARS

Only three days had elapsed between the assassination of President John F. Kennedy on Nov. 22, 1963, and the first notice from the director of the Mint to the chief engraver to prepare for the issue of a coin bearing his portrait. Gilroy Roberts fashioned its obverse portrait based on the Kennedy inaugural medal to save time. The reverse is Frank Gasparro's rendition of the presidential seal. Remarkably, working dies were ready by January 2. Kennedy halves have been struck in three different compositions. The 1964 issue was struck in the traditional 90-percent silver alloy. The following year, when dimes and quarters were changed to cupro-nickel clad copper, the half dollar was preserved as a silver alloy coin by striking it in a silver clad version containing 80-percent silver in its outer layers, and 21-percent silver in its middle layer. The remaining alloy was copper. Finally, silver was abandoned in 1971, and only sporadic collector issues have been struck in that metal since. Circulation issues are now struck in the same clad composition as dimes and quarters. Coins dated 1970D,

1987P and 1987D were not issued to circulation, but are widely available from broken up mint sets.

A special reverse was used in 1975 and 1976 (both with 1976 obverse) to commemorate the American Bicentennial. It depicts Independence Hall in Philadelphia designed by Seth G. Huntington.

★ ★ **COUNTERFEIT ALERT** ★ ★

It is possible that none exist.

1964 Kennedy Half Dollar with Presidential Seal Reverse

	MS-65
1964	9.00
1964D	9.00

SILVER CLAD

	MS-65
1965	4.50
1966	4.50
1967	4.50
1968D	4.50
1968S, *proof only*	7.00
1969D	4.50
1969S, *proof only*	7.00
1970D	13.00
1970S, *proof only*	19.50

CUPRO-NICKEL CLAD COPPER

	MS-65
1971	2.00
1971D	2.00
1971S, *proof only*	5.00
1972	2.00
1972D	2.00
1972S, *proof only*	5.50
1973	2.00
1973D	2.00
1973S, *proof only*	5.50
1974	2.00
1974D	2.00
1974S, *proof only*	4.00

1976D Kennedy Half Dollar with Bicentennial Reverse

BICENTENNIAL REVERSE

	MS-65
1976, Bicentennial	2.00
1976D, Bicentennial	2.00
1976S, Bicentennial, *proof only*	5.00
1976S, Bicentennial, Silver Clad	4.50
1977	2.00
1977D	2.00
1977S, *proof only*	4.50
1978	4.00
1978D	4.00
1978S, *proof only*	3.00
1979	2.00
1979D	2.00
1979, filled S, *proof only*	3.00
1979, clear S, *proof only*	18.50
1980P	2.00
1980D	2.00
1980S, *proof only*	2.50
1981P	2.00
1981D	2.00
1981S, *proof only*	2.50
1982P	3.50
1982D	3.50
1982S, *proof only*	3.00
1983P	3.50
1983D	3.50
1983S, *proof only*	3.00
1984P	3.00
1984D	3.00
1984S, *proof only*	3.50
1985P	3.00
1985D	3.00
1985S, *proof only*	4.00

	MS-65
1986P	3.50
1986D	3.50
1986S, *proof only*	7.50
1987P	4.00
1987D	4.00
1987S, *proof only*	4.00
1988P	3.50
1988D	3.50
1988S, *proof only*	6.50
1989P	2.50
1989D	2.50
1989S, *proof only*	7.00
1990P	3.00
1990D	3.00
1990S, *proof only*	5.00
1991P	3.50
1991D	3.50
1991S, *proof only*	11.50
1992P	2.50
1992D	3.50
1992S, *proof only*	7.50
1992S, Silver, *proof only*	15.00
1993P	3.00
1993D	4.00
1993S, *proof only*	14.00
1993S, Silver, *proof only*	27.00
1994P	2.00
1994D	2.00
1994S, *proof only*	9.00
1994S, Silver, *proof only*	35.00
1995P	2.00
1995D	2.00

	MS-65			MS-65
1995S, *proof only*	45.00	2002P	3.00
1995S, Silver, *proof only*	100.00	2002D	3.00
1996P	2.00	2002S, *proof only*	10.00
1996D	2.00	2002S, Silver, *proof only*	13.50
1996S, *proof only*	10.50	2003P	2.50
1996S, Silver, *proof only*	50.00	2003D	2.50
1997P	2.00	2003S, *proof only*	7.00
1997D	2.00	2003S, Silver, *proof only*	12.50
1997S, *proof only*	26.00	2004P	2.00
1997S, Silver, *proof only*	95.00	2004D	2.00
1998P	2.00	2004S, *proof only*	12.00
1998D	2.00	2004S, Silver, *proof only*	11.00
1998S, *proof only*	15.00	2005P	2.00
1998S, Matte, *proof only*	350.00	2005D	2.00
1998S, Silver, *proof only*	30.00	2005S, *proof only*	9.50
1999P	2.25	2005S, Silver, *proof only*	12.50
1999D	2.25	2006P	2.00
1999S, *proof only*	18.00	2006D	2.00
1999S, Silver, *proof only*	35.00	2006S, *proof only*	7.00
2000P	2.50	2006S, Silver, *proof only*	12.50
2000D	2.50	2007P	2.00
2000S, *proof only*	5.00	2007D	2.00
2000S, Silver, *proof only*	12.50	2007S, *proof only*	7.00
2001P	2.50	2007S, Silver, *proof only*	12.50
2001D	2.50	2008P	2.50
2001S, *proof only*	10.00	2008D	2.50
2001S, Silver, *proof only*	18.50	2008S, *proof only*	7.50
		2008S, Silver, *proof only*	13.50

EARLY SILVER DOLLARS

The first American silver dollar was intended to fill the same role in commerce as the old Spanish colonial milled dollar. The dollar, along with the half dollar and half dime, was one of the first silver denominations to be released by the new United States Mint. As a result, it first appeared with the briefly used flowing hair design. These first rare pieces were struck in 1794 and 1795 on crude blanks, often exhibiting "adjustment marks" from the filing off of excess silver before striking.

While considered part of the manufacturing process, these marks nevertheless reduce the value of a specimen. The initial reverse design, showing a rather skinny eagle within a wreath, continued to be used after the flowing hair obverse was replaced by the rather voluptuous draped bust design. After four years of use this eagle was replaced with a plumper eagle carrying a heraldic shield.

As with the smaller denominations, the government's lack of bullion and skilled labor made it impossible to strike enough pieces to have a significant role in the economy. Another complication soon ended the life of the silver dollar altogether. The average silver content of these coins slightly exceeded that of the Spanish dollar, though it was exchangeable for them at par. Most of them were thus exported and melted, with worn Spanish dollars being shipped back in their place. Not willing to change the dollar's specifications, the government simply ceased to strike it for 30 years! During the last year they were struck for circulation (1804) only old dies, probably dated 1803, were used. In the 1830s, when a few dollars were needed as gifts for foreign heads of state, the Mint struck bust dollars appearing like what the 1804 dollars *would* have looked like if they had borne that date. These exceedingly rare "1804" dollars have become among the most famous United States coins. A small number were also restruck somewhat later for collectors.

Rare die combinations of early coins can command a premium from specialists.

★ ★ COUNTERFEIT ALERT ★ ★

It is likely that all dates of early dollars have been counterfeited. Some of the cruder counterfeits can be easily distinguished by the plain or reeded edges they have, as opposed to the lettered edges of the authentic pieces. Other counterfeits are more dangerous. A false 1794 is known re-engraved from a real 1795. A great many counterfeit 1804s exist. Holed coins are sometimes deceptively plugged. Cleaning is a frequent problem, both on real and counterfeit pieces. On the latter it can sometimes make authentication more difficult.

FLOWING HAIR TYPE

	VG	VF
1794	**90,000.00**	**160,000.00**

	VG	VF
1795	**5,600.00**	**19,000.00**

1795 Silver Dollar with Flowing Hair

DRAPED BUST/SMALL EAGLE

	VG	VF
1795	**1,750.00**	**4,650.00**
1796	**1,750.00**	**4,800.00**
1797, 9 & 7 stars, small letters	**2,750.00**	**8,000.00**
1797, 9 & 7 stars, large letters	**1,825.00**	**5,200.00**

	VG	VF
1797, 10 stars l. & 6 stars r.	**1,775.00**	**4,700.00**
1798, 15 stars	**2,150.00**	**5,800.00**
1798, 13 stars	**1,650.00**	**4,900.00**

1795 Silver Dollar with Draped Bust and Small Eagle

1798 Silver Dollar with Draped Bust and Heraldic Eagle

DRAPED BUST/HERALDIC EAGLE

	VG	VF
1798	1,000.00	2,450.00
1799, 9 over 8, 15 stars	1,100.00	2,800.00
1799, 9 over 8, 13 stars	1,100.00	2,850.00
1799	975.00	2,400.00
1799, 8 stars l. & 5 stars r.	1,200.00	3,000.00
1800	975.00	2,400.00
1801	1,100.00	2,800.00
1802, 2 over 1	1,100.00	2,800.00
1802	1,050.00	2,700.00
1802, *proof restrike*	—	250,000.00
1803	1,050.00	2,500.00
1803, *proof restrike*	—	250,000.00
1804, (struck 1834-35), *proof*	—	4,100,000.00
1804, (struck 1859), *proof*	—	1,200,000.00

GOBRECHT DOLLARS

It is ironic that the coin for which the Seated Liberty design was first prepared was the last to have it appear on pieces actively struck for circulation. It was the intent that when the striking of silver dollars was resumed, a design of exceptional artistic merit be used. For this reason, Christian Gobrecht was asked to prepare dies based on a drawing of Liberty seated by artist Thomas Sully. It is generally accepted that his seated goddess concept of Liberty derives from depictions of the Roman allegory of Britannia on British coins. The reverse design was also a radical departure from the staid old heraldic eagle. The new eagle was seen in the realistic attitude of flight. It was prepared by Gobrecht based on a drawing of "Old Pete" by the famous Titian Peale. Old Pete was an eagle who lived at the Mint ca.1830-36, and who met an unfortunate end, getting caught in the machinery. While Gobrecht dollars are not all patterns, very few were ever struck for circulation, never more than 1,000 or so of any one variety. Only circulating issues are listed here. Pattern pieces with the engraver's name in the field as opposed to on the base, as well as 1838 issues, are listed in that section. Later, some were restruck for collectors. These can usually be distinguished by the misaligned dies which make the eagle appear to be flying horizontally when the coin is turned around. Originals have the eagle flying slightly upward.

★ ★ COUNTERFEIT ALERT ★ ★

Gobrecht experimental dollars are less often counterfeited than other early dollars. Cleaning and polishing are problems.

1836 Gobrecht Dollar with Stars on Reverse

STARS ON REVERSE

	VF	XF		VF	XF
1836, (coin alignment)	8,500.00	12,000.00	1836, (struck 1837, medal alignment)	8,500.00	12,000.00

1839 Gobrecht Dollar with Stars on Obverse

STARS ON OBVERSE

	VF	XF
1839	**15,000.00**	**20,000.00**

SEATED LIBERTY DOLLARS

The active production of silver dollars was finally resumed in 1840. However, the reverse design especially created for them was replaced by a more mundane heraldic eagle, similar to that in use on the minor coinage. While production of these coins continued for most years, those struck from 1853 to about 1867 were primarily intended as bullion pieces for export, each containing more than a dollar's worth of silver. A ribbon with the motto "In God We Trust" was added over the eagle in 1866. These dollars are often found cleaned. Be careful of retoned specimens as well.

★ ★ COUNTERFEIT ALERT ★ ★

Counterfeits of this type are not common.

NO MOTTO ABOVE EAGLE

	F	XF		F	XF
1840	325.00	. . . 600.00	1846	280.00	. . . 550.00
1841	295.00	. . . 425.00	1846O	320.00	. . . 750.00
1842	295.00	. . . 425.00	1847	275.00	. . . 425.00
1843	295.00	. . . 400.00	1848	480.00	. . . 900.00
1844	300.00	. . . 550.00	1849	280.00	. . . 480.00
1845	385.00	. . . 600.00	1850	700.00	. 1,300.00

1845 Seated Liberty Dollar with No Motto Above Eagle

	F	XF
1850O	475.00	1,500.00
1851, original	8,000.00	14,500.00
1851, restrike proof	—	54,000.00
1852, original	6,500.00	11,500.00
1852, restrike proof	—	56,000.00
1853	545.00	850.00
1854	1,900.00	3,800.00
1855	1,400.00	3,600.00
1856	600.00	1,250.00
1857	575.00	1,250.00
1858	4,000.00	5,600.00

	F	XF
1859	400.00	675.00
1859O	300.00	485.00
1859S	490.00	1,750.00
1860	385.00	575.00
1860O	300.00	445.00
1861	950.00	1,350.00
1862	900.00	1,300.00
1863	575.00	1,300.00
1864	500.00	700.00
1865	400.00	775.00
1866		two known

1872 Seated Liberty Dollar with Motto Above Eagle

MOTTO ABOVE EAGLE

	F	XF
1866	350.00	600.00
1867	330.00	600.00
1868	325.00	575.00

	F	XF
1869	300.00	475.00
1870	300.00	475.00
1870CC	750.00	1,750.00

	F	XF
1870S	98,000.00	275,000.00
1871	265.00	425.00
1871CC	4,000.00	10,500.00
1872	275.00	450.00
1872CC	2,400.00	5,500.00

	F	XF
1872S	450.00	1,600.00
1873	300.00	475.00
1873CC	6,500.00	17,500.00
1873S		none known to exist

TRADE DOLLARS

Trade dollars were coins struck deliberately for export as bullion, usually to the Far East. They were chiefly intended to compete against the Mexican peso, which had slightly more silver than a standard dollar. They were distinguished by a Liberty and eagle facing the opposite direction from the standard dollars. From the very beginning their legal tender status was limited in the United States. But in 1876, when the price of silver dropped, they ceased to have legal tender altogether, not having it restored until 1965! Eight million were redeemed by the government in 1887. Any struck between 1879 and 1885 are proof-only collectors' issues. Prices listed for them are for circulated examples.

It was typical for Oriental merchants to impress a character into these and other silver coins, to confirm that they accepted them as good quality. These "chop marks" are commonly found on trade dollars, sometimes in quantity. They reduce the value of the coin as a form of mutilation, but have recently been the subject of serious research. Chop marked dollars may not be as valuable, but are still collectible.

★ ★ COUNTERFEIT ALERT ★ ★

Recently, VG base metal counterfeits based in Communist China have been plentiful. Older contemporary counterfeits also exist. Be cautious of cleaned coins.

1876 Trade Dollar

	F	XF		F	XF
1873	145.00	260.00	1877	140.00	180.00
1873CC	320.00	900.00	1877CC	300.00	580.00
1873S	160.00	275.00	1877S	138.00	180.00
1874	160.00	275.00	1878, proof only	—	3,500.00
1874CC	300.00	475.00	1878CC	700.00	2,350.00
1874S	140.00	200.00	1878S	138.00	180.00
1875	375.00	600.00	1879, proof only	—	3,500.00
1875CC	250.00	400.00	1880, proof only	—	3,500.00
1875S	140.00	200.00	1881, proof only	—	3,500.00
1875S, S over CC	400.00	900.00	1882, proof only	—	3,500.00
1876	140.00	200.00	1883, proof only	—	3,500.00
1876CC	285.00	430.00	1884, proof only	—	10 known
1876S	138.00	180.00	1885, proof only	—	five known

MORGAN DOLLARS

The Morgan dollar was introduced as a result of pressure from the silver mining lobby. For decades, silver dollars had been scarce in circulation. With the boom in silver mining, the price of the metal dropped as more became available. Something needed to be done to remove the excess silver from the market. The new design coincided with the reintroduction of the silver dollar. Because they were inconvenient, many, perhaps hundreds of thousands of these dollars, sat for decades in bags, held as private, bank, and government reserves. The U.S. Treasury was stuck with such an excess that thousands remained on hand for almost a century, prompting the famous GSA auction of silver dollars in the 1970s. Those coins in distinctive GSA cases often command a slight premium.

Artistically, many consider the Morgan dollar, named after its designer, George T. Morgan, an aesthetically pleasing but unoriginal design. Morgan's competence (and perhaps his interesting use of Gothic script) may perhaps be attributed to his training at the Royal Mint in London. A long gap exists between 1904 and the last Morgan issue in 1921. During this time the master dies were lost and new ones had to be prepared. As a result, there are subtle differences of relief in the 1921 issue. It is less pleasing and dealer "bids" are often less for that year than for other bulk Morgan dollars. Another subtle variation in the appearance of Morgan dollars is the variation in quality of strike from mint to mint. San Francisco-made examples are usually fully struck, Philadelphia are medium, and New Orleans dollars are usually the most weakly struck. The eagle's breast on high-grade pieces is usually the spot where these differences are most obvious.

Morgans have been among the most popular coins to invest in. This is partially due to their availability in great quantities in uncirculated condition, the typical grade favored by investment promoters and the mass of investors. It is ironic that their sheer commonness has contributed to their desirability.

★ ★ COUNTERFEIT ALERT ★ ★

Genuine coins have been known altered to pass for 1879CC, 1889CC, 1892S, 1893S, 1894, 1895, 1895S, 1896S, 1901, 1903S, and 1904S dates. Cast counterfeits are known of 1878, 1878S, 1879S, 1880O, 1881, 1883, 1883S, 1885, 1888O, 1889, 1889O, 1892O, 1899O, 1901, 1902, 1903, 1904S, 1921D, and 1921S. Struck counterfeits of certain rare dates are also possible. Cleaned coins are common and are heavily discounted, as are scuffed and heavily edge-knocked pieces. Be careful to avoid coins with false toning.

1881CC Morgan Dollar

	VF	MS-60
1878, 8 tail feathers	38.00	130.00
1878, 7 over 8 tail feathers	28.00	150.00
1878, 7 feathers	26.00	75.00
1878, 7 feathers, rev. of 1879	24.00	82.00
1878CC	115.00	230.00
1878S	26.00	60.00
1879	24.00	37.00

	VF	MS-60
1879CC	300.00	4,350.00
1879O	24.00	80.00
1879S	24.00	40.00
1880	24.00	37.00
1880CC	220.00	580.00
1880O	24.00	65.00
1880S	24.00	38.00
1881	24.00	38.00
1881CC	450.00	575.00

	VF	MS-60
1881O	24.00	37.00
1881S	24.00	37.00
1882	24.00	37.00
1882CC	120.00	230.00
1882O	24.00	40.50
1882O, O over S	40.00	260.00
1882S	24.00	37.00
1883	24.00	37.00
1883CC	120.00	220.00
1883O	24.00	37.00
1883S	24.00	635.00
1884	24.00	37.00
1884CC	160.00	215.00
1884O	24.00	37.00

	VF	MS-60
1884S	24.00	6,000.00
1885	24.00	37.00
1885CC	600.00	660.00
1885O	24.00	37.00
1885S	40.00	245.00
1886	24.00	37.00
1886O	25.00	700.00
1886S	85.00	330.00
1887, 7 over 6	35.00	450.00
1887	24.00	37.00
1887O, 7 over 6	36.00	350.00
1887O	25.00	55.00
1887S	26.00	115.00
1888	24.00	37.00

1887O Morgan Dollar

	VF	MS-60
1888O	24.00	37.00
1888S	215.00	310.00
1889	24.00	37.00
1889CC	1,750.00	23,000.00
1889O	25.00	140.00
1889S	70.00	215.00
1890	24.00	37.00
1890CC	115.00	460.00
1890O	25.00	58.00
1890S	24.00	58.00
1891	24.00	55.00
1891CC	120.00	375.00
1891O	24.00	140.00
1891S	24.00	60.00
1892	27.00	165.00

	VF	MS-60
1892CC	315.00	1,700.00
1892O	26.00	170.00
1892S	135.00	36,000.00
1893	270.00	800.00
1893CC	335.00	3,800.00
1893O	400.00	2,300.00
1893S	7,500.00	85,000.00
1894	1,900.00	5,000.00
1894O	75.00	600.00
1894S	110.00	700.00
1895, *proof only*	—	50,000.00
1895O	620.00	18,000.00
1895S	600.00	4,250.00
1896	24.00	37.00
1896O	24.50	1,450.00

1892S Morgan Dollar

1901 Morgan Dollar

	VF	MS-60		VF	MS-60
1896S	60.00	1,775.00	1901O	24.00	37.00
1897	24.00	37.00	1901S	32.00	470.00
1897O	25.00	800.00	1902	24.00	45.00
1897S	24.00	60.00	1902O	24.00	37.00
1898	24.00	37.00	1902S	160.00	450.00
1898O	24.00	37.00	1903	55.00	77.50
1898S	36.00	270.00	1903O	380.00	450.00
1899	215.00	325.00	1903S	210.00	4,700.00
1899O	24.00	37.00	1904	30.00	80.00
1899S	40.00	325.00	1904O	27.00	38.00
1900	24.00	37.00	1904S	95.00	1,350.00
1900O	24.00	37.00	1921	19.00	25.50
1900O, O over CC	65.00	370.00	1921D	19.00	45.00
1900S	27.00	350.00	1921S	19.00	35.00
1901	60.00	2,200.00			

PEACE DOLLARS

Like the Morgan dollar before it, the Peace dollar was the result of Congressional authorization for a new large coinage of silver dollars. When the famous numismatist Farran Zerbe learned that this new issue of dollars was to bear the old Morgan design, he agitated for a new, artistically more progressive replacement. This was to be a new radiant Liberty head by sculptor Anthony de Francisci. It was not only in harmony with the new designs for the other denominations, especially those by Weinman and St. Gaudens, but also commemorated the end of World War I. The word "PEACE" can be seen upon the rocky perch on which the eagle stands. The very first Peace dollars, those struck in 1921 only, were struck in a much higher relief. Later issues have a lower relief more suitable to mass production. The old silver dollar was last made for circulation in 1935. The Peace dollar out-lived this death sentence for 30 years in the form of the mysterious issue of 1964. While none have been officially verified, there have long been rumors, generally accepted by the numismatic community, that several escaped the Mint's melting pot.

Like the Morgan dollar, this coin is available in mint-state in abundant quantities. The broad smooth surfaces, however, permit many mint-state pieces to reveal unsightly bruises and bag marks.

★ ★ COUNTERFEIT ALERT ★ ★

1928 altered from 1923 or 1928S, as well as other counterfeits of this date.

1921 Peace Dollar

	VF	MS-60
1921	140.00	250.00
1922	18.50	22.00
1922D	18.50	27.00
1922S	18.50	27.00
1923	18.50	21.00
1923D	19.00	53.00
1923S	18.50	30.00
1924	18.50	21.00
1924S	31.00	215.00
1925	18.50	21.00
1925S	25.00	75.00
1926	18.50	40.00
1926D	18.50	66.00

	VF	MS-60
1926S	18.50	40.00
1927	35.00	70.00
1927D	35.00	150.00
1927S	35.00	150.00
1928	455.00	530.00
1928S	40.00	160.00
1934	21.50	105.00
1934D	22.50	135.00
1934S	90.00	1,800.00
1935	22.00	62.00
1935S	21.00	250.00
1964D	*No confirmed examples known.*	

EISENHOWER DOLLARS

The "Ike" dollar was struck as much to commemorate the first manned moon landing in 1969, as to honor President Dwight D. Eisenhower. The reverse of this coin was an adaptation of the Apollo XI insignia, depicting an eagle clutching an olive branch and landing on the moon. The obverse shows a left-facing portrait of Eisenhower. Circulation strikes were of the same cupro-nickel clad composition as the dime and quarter. Special collectors' issues were also struck in a silver clad version similar to the alloy used for the half dollars of 1965-1970. These special silver coins bearing the "S" mintmark were released in blue envelopes for the uncirculated issues, and brown boxes for the proofs. Most dealers and collectors require that they be in the original packaging.

A special reverse was used to commemorate the Bicentennial. It featured the Liberty Bell superimposed on the moon, as arranged by design contest winner Dennis R. Williams. While all Bicentennial dollars are dated "1776-1976," they were struck in both 1975 and 1976. The reverse of the former uses heavy block lettering, the latter mostly used slightly finer letters. They are easily identified by the lack of copper on the reeded edge.

★ ★ COUNTERFEIT ALERT ★ ★

Poor quality counterfeits have recently come out of Communist China. Specifically, 1976D is known.

1974D Eisenhower Dollar with Eagle Reverse

	MS-63	PRF-65
1971	—	10.00
1971D	—	5.00
1971S, Silver	8.00	11.00
1972	—	6.00
1972D	—	5.50
1972S, Silver	8.00	12.00
1973	—	14.00

	MS-63	PRF-65
1973D	—	15.00
1973S, proof only	—	12.00
1973S, Silver	8.50	32.00
1974	—	5.50
1974D	—	6.00
1974S, proof only	—	10.00
1974S, Silver	8.00	7.25

1976D Eisenhower Dollar with Bicentennial on Reverse

BICENTENNIAL REVERSE

	MS-63	PRF-65
1976, block letters	—	9.50
1976, finer letters	—	5.00
1976D, block letters	—	6.00
1976D, finer letters	—	5.00
1976S, block letters, proof only	—	13.00
1976S, finer letters, proof only	—	9.00
1976S, Silver, block letters	13.00	20.00

REGULAR ISSUE CONTINUED

	MS-63	PRF-65
1977	—	7.50
1977D	—	7.50
1977S, *proof only*	—	9.50
1978	—	5.00
1978D	—	5.00
1978S, *proof only*	—	12.00

SUSAN B. ANTHONY DOLLARS

The Anthony "mini-dollar" was struck to achieve two specific ends. It was intended to save the government money by replacing the quickly worn out one-dollar bill with a coin which would last in circulation for decades. It was also a coin greatly supported and pushed for by the vending machine lobby. The large Ike dollars were inconvenient for vending machines, but a coin of its value was necessary to facilitate the sale of more expensive items in such machines.

Its obverse depicts Frank Gasparro's portrait of Susan B. Anthony, who was instrumental in gaining women the right to vote. The reverse design is the same Apollo XI motif as on the Eisenhower dollar.

Certainly one of the least popular coins in the history of the United States, it was far too close in diameter to the quarter, with which it was frequently confused. It was of the same clad composition. The third year of issue (1981) was not even placed into circulation, and was just obtainable in mint sets. The final year (1999) was only struck in anticipation of its immediate replacement by the Sacagawea dollar.

★ ★ COUNTERFEIT ALERT ★ ★

Not common.

1979D Susan B. Anthony Dollar

	MS-63	PRF-65
1979P, narrow rim, far date	—	2.50
1979P, wide rim, near date	—	60.00
1979D	—	3.00
1979S	—	3.00
1979S, filled S	—	8.00
1979S, clear S	—	110.00
1980	—	3.00

	MS-63	PRF-65
1980D	—	2.00
1980S	3.50	8.00
1981	—	8.00
1981D	—	8.00
1981S	—	8.00
1981S, filled S	—	8.00
1981S, clear S	—	230.00
1999P	4.00	30.00
1999D	—	4.00

SACAGAWEA DOLLARS

Despite the failure of the SBA to win any amount of popular acceptance at all, the reasons why it was originally issued remained. The government could save millions by replacing the dollar bill with a more durable coin. Also, a dollar coin of moderate size was still sought by the vending machine industry to facilitate the sale of more expensive items.

The confusion caused by the Anthony dollar was eliminated by changing the color, and giving the new coin a broad border. This new, well-designed coin depicts Sacagawea, the Shoshone Indian guide and translator who accompanied the Lewis and Clark expedition to explore the Northwest (1804-06). She carries her infant son on her back. It is the work of Glenna Goodacre. The reverse, designed by Thomas D. Rogers, Jr., depicts a graceful eagle in flight.

While it is the same size as the Anthony dollar, it has a unique composition. It is a brass of 77-percent copper, 12-percent zinc, seven-percent manganese, and four-percent nickel, bonded to a pure copper core. This coin is prone to spotting. Mint-state examples lacking spots are more desirable.

★ ★ COUNTERFEIT ALERT ★ ★

Quantities are known, primarily made for circulation in Ecuador.

2002P Sacagawea Dollar

	MS-63	PRF-65		MS-63	PRF-65
2000P	—	2.00	2001S	—	95.00
2000D	—	2.00	2002P	—	2.00
2000S	—	10.00	2002D	—	2.00
2001P	—	4.00	2002S	—	28.50
2001D	—	4.00	2003P	—	2.50

	MS-63	PF		MS-63	PF
2003D	—	2.50	2006P	—	2.50
2003S	—	12.50	2006D	—	2.50
2004P	—	2.50	2006S	—	22.50
2004D	—	2.50	2007P	—	2.50
2004S	—	22.50	2007D	—	2.50
2005P	—	2.50	2007S	—	22.50
2005D	—	2.50	2008P	—	2.50
2005S	—	22.50	2008D	—	2.50
			2008S	—	22.50

PRESIDENTIAL DOLLARS

Following on the heels of the very popular Statehood quarters, Congress authorized the Mint to embark on a 10-plus year program of Presidential dollars, which would depict a different president every three months, each in chronological order. The reverse depicts the Statue of Liberty. The composition of these dollars is the same as that of the Sacagawea dollar.

One innovation of this series is their incuse lettered edge. Occasionally, lettered edges have been used on American coins, but most have been raised, not incuse. More unusual is the fact that not only is the motto on the edge, but that one must look there to find the date and mintmark.

The edges of these quickly proved to be very susceptible to errors of various sorts, most often doubling. These errors have attracted much public attention. Prices for them soared just a few weeks. However, not all dealers are even willing to buy them. Many are concerned that these high prices reflect no more than a passing fad.

Presidential dollars are collected almost exclusively in mint-state condition. So far, counterfeits have not plagued this series, despite the interest in the unusual edges.

GEORGE WASHINGTON

	MS-63
2007P	.2.00
2007D	.2.00
2007S, *proof only*	.5.00
ND (2007), plain edge error	**75.00**

JOHN ADAMS

	MS-63
2007P	.2.00
2007P, dbl. edge lettering	**125.00**
2007D	.2.00
2007S, *proof only*	.5.00

THOMAS JEFFERSON

	MS-63
2007P	.2.00
2007D	.2.00
2007S, *proof only*	.5.00

JAMES MADISON

	MS-63
2007P	.2.00
2007D	.2.00
2007S, *proof only*	.5.00

JAMES MONROE

	MS-63
2008P	2.00
2008D	2.00
2008S, *proof only*	5.00

JOHN QUINCY ADAMS

	MS-63
2008P	2.00
2008D	2.00
2008S, *proof only*	5.00

ANDREW JACKSON

	MS-63
2008P	2.00
2008D	2.00
2008S, *proof only*	5.00

MARTIN VAN BUREN

	MS-63
2008P	2.00
2008D	2.00
2008S, *proof only*	5.00

ONE-DOLLAR GOLD PIECES

Although the gold dollar was originally planned as early as 1791, and patterns were prepared in 1836, it was not until 1849 that they were finally approved. Earlier demand was being filled by privately struck Georgia and Carolina gold of standard United States coinage weight, and the Mint director personally opposed their issue. When Congressional intervention was coupled with the new flow of gold from California, the Mint had to give in. The first gold dollars, designed as one of James Longacre's early projects, were a mere 12.7 mm. in diameter and were easily lost. The diameter was increased to 14.3 mm., and the coin was thinned in 1854 to make them easier to handle, but the new narrow head design was of too high relief and parts of the date on the reverse did not always strike up. The gold dollar's final modification came in 1856, when the wide flan was retained but a lower-relief portrait of Liberty similar to that on the Three Dollar piece was used.

Many gold dollars were used at the time in jewelry and bear solder marks, especially the first type. These coins are worth a fraction of the value of unmutilated coins. Mutilated examples are far more common than worn ones, with few examples grading lower than VF.

★ ★ COUNTERFEIT ALERT ★ ★

1849C open wreath and 1854C exist, made by altering genuine coins of other dates or mints. Cast counterfeits have been made of 1850-54. It is important to note that struck counterfeits exist of virtually every date in this series.

1849 Dollar Gold Piece with Coronet (Type I)

CORONET HEAD—TYPE I

	VF	XF
1849, open wreath	175.00	220.00
1849, closed wreath	175.00	200.00
1849C, open wreath	*extremely rare*	
1849C, closed wreath	1,200.00	1,950.00
1849D	1,400.00	2,100.00
1849O	180.00	265.00
1850	175.00	200.00
1850C	1,150.00	1,800.00
1850D	1,250.00	2,000.00
1850O	280.00	400.00
1851	175.00	200.00
1851C	995.00	1,300.00
1851D	1,150.00	1,600.00
1851O	175.00	225.00
1852	175.00	200.00
1852C	1,150.00	1,300.00
1852D	1,250.00	1,600.00
1852O	190.00	250.00
1853	175.00	200.00
1853C	1,100.00	1,600.00
1853D	1,250.00	1,750.00
1853O	175.00	235.00
1854	175.00	200.00
1854D	1,400.00	2,400.00
1854S	375.00	550.00

1854 Dollar Gold Piece with Narrow Indian Princess Head - Type II

NARROW INDIAN PRINCESS HEAD—TYPE II

	VF	XF
1854	320.00	450.00
1855	320.00	450.00
1855C	1,500.00	4,000.00
1855D	5,000.00	12,000.00
1855O	440.00	600.00
1856S	925.00	1,325.00

1860D Dollar Gold Piece with Large Indian Princess Head - Type III

LARGE INDIAN PRINCESS HEAD— TYPE III

	VF	XF		VF	XF
1856, upright 5	185.00	215.00	1867	400.00	525.00
1856, slanted 5	185.00	210.00	1868	295.00	415.00
1856D	3,900.00	6,000.00	1869	335.00	530.00
1857	185.00	210.00	1870	285.00	400.00
1857C	1,150.00	1,750.00	1870S	500.00	800.00
1857D	1,400.00	2,750.00	1871	285.00	400.00
1857S	550.00	750.00	1872	275.00	400.00
1858	185.00	210.00	1873, closed 3	425.00	820.00
1858D	1,250.00	1,650.00	1873, open 3	185.00	210.00
1858S	425.00	600.00	1874	185.00	210.00
1859	185.00	210.00	1875	2,350.00	3,850.00
1859C	1,050.00	1,700.00	1876	275.00	350.00
1859D	1,400.00	1,800.00	1877	185.00	345.00
1859S	250.00	600.00	1878	250.00	350.00
1860	185.00	210.00	1879	225.00	325.00
1860D	3,000.00	4,000.00	1880	185.00	210.00
1860S	380.00	500.00	1881	185.00	210.00
1861	185.00	210.00	1882	185.00	215.00
1861D, (struck by the Confederacy)	8,000.00	13,500.00	1883	185.00	210.00
1862	185.00	210.00	1884	185.00	210.00
1863	500.00	925.00	1885	185.00	215.00
1864	350.00	440.00	1886	185.00	215.00
1865	350.00	575.00	1887	185.00	210.00
1866	360.00	475.00	1888	185.00	210.00
			1889	185.00	210.00

2-1/2-DOLLAR GOLD PIECES

The first strikes of the quarter eagle (gold 2-1/2-dollar piece) came the year following the first introduction of American gold coinage, the half eagle and eagle preceding it in 1795. However, it preceded the other denominations as being the first coin to depict the heraldic eagle bearing a shield on its chest, which later was featured on all denominations other than copper. Its first obverse features a bust of Liberty wearing a tall conical cap, traditionally but inaccurately referred to by numismatists as a turban. This first bust by Robert Scott was replaced by one designed by John Reich, and had a smaller cap. A reverse eagle similar, but more realistic, was paired with the new obverse. A large gap in the striking of quarter eagles followed immediately upon the release of this new design, which was finally restored on the same standard but at a slightly smaller diameter in 1821.

Through most of its history until the 1830s, the quarter eagle was plagued by mass meltings, because it was undervalued relative to its gold content, particularly by European standards. In 1834, this was remedied by reducing the coin's gold content. This was indicated to the public by the removal of the motto over the eagle on the reverse, and by a new capless Liberty head, the "Classic Head" by William Kneass. The final Coronet-type Liberty head design was a rendition by Christian Gobrecht, which continued in use from 1840 to 1907 without change. Those 1848 pieces, countermarked "CAL.," were struck with gold shipped east by the military governor of California.

In 1908, as part of the same coin design beautification program which later introduced the Walking Liberty half dollar and St. Gaudens double eagle, sculptor Bela Lyon Pratt was asked to prepare new designs for the quarter and half eagle in secret under the authority of President Theodore Roosevelt. His work showed the bust of an Indian chief on the obverse and an eagle with closed wings on the reverse. It was both controversial and innovative in that it bore its design in relief, but recessed below the surface of the coin. While some criticized it both for aesthetic reasons and for fear of it spreading germs in dirt trapped in the recesses, it proved to be a very successful method of shielding the design from wear.

★ ★ COUNTERFEIT ALERT ★ ★

Examples of 1848 CAL., 1875, and 1911D exist by altering genuine coins of other dates or mints. Struck counterfeits exist of virtually every date in this series. All examples of 1905S are counterfeit—no real ones exist. Be cautious of false C mintmarks altered by cutting down an authentic O mintmark. Beware of traces of solder on earlier coins from use as jewelry. Look for interruption in the pattern of edge reeding. Be cautious of cleaned coins. This is harder to detect on gold, which usually does not tone naturally.

1807 2-1/2-Dollar Gold Piece with Turban Bust

TURBAN BUST RIGHT

	F	XF		F	XF
1796, no stars on obverse	35,000.00	75,000.00	1804, 13 stars	24,500.00	75,000.00
1796, stars	30,000.00	65,000.00	1804, 14 stars	5,000.00	10,000.00
1797	17,000.00	30,000.00	1805	6,000.00	10,000.00
1798	6,500.00	13,000.00	1806, 6 over 4	5,750.00	10,500.00
1802, 2 over 1	5,000.00	10,000.00	1806, 6 over 5	9,000.00	18,500.00
			1807	5,500.00	10,000.00

1831 2-1/2-Dollar Gold Piece with Capped Bust

CAPPED BUST TYPE

	F	XF		F	XF
1808	29,500.00	55,000.00	1829	5,000.00	7,500.00
1821	6,000.00	8,000.00	1830	5,000.00	7,500.00
1824, 4 over 1	6,000.00	8,000.00	1831	5,000.00	7,500.00
1825	6,000.00	8,000.00	1832	5,000.00	7,500.00
1826, 6 over 5	6,250.00	10,500.00	1833	5,000.00	7,600.00
1827	6,000.00	9,500.00	1834	9,000.00	16,500.00

1834 2-1/2-Dollar Gold Piece with Classic Head (No Motto)

CLASSIC HEAD (NO MOTTO)

	VF	XF		VF	XF
1834	270.00	800.00	1838C	1,400.00	3,000.00
1835	270.00	800.00	1839	400.00	1,500.00
1836	270.00	800.00	1839C	1,400.00	3,200.00
1837	300.00	950.00	1839D	1,350.00	4,000.00
1838	300.00	800.00	1839O	500.00	1,300.00

1842O 2-1/2-Dollar Gold Piece with Coronet (No Motto)

CORONET TYPE (NO MOTTO)

	VF	XF
1840	160.00	850.00
1840C	1,000.00	1,800.00
1840D	2,100.00	8,800.00
1840O	225.00	800.00
1841	—	87,500.00
1841C	800.00	2,000.00
1841D	1,200.00	4,850.00
1842	450.00	2,900.00
1842C	900.00	3,600.00
1842D	1,000.00	4,350.00
1842O	240.00	1,200.00
1843	165.00	475.00
1843C, crosslet 4, small date	1,600.00	5,600.00
1843C, plain 4, large date	850.00	2,200.00
1843D	990.00	2,350.00
1843O, crosslet 4, small date	165.00	250.00
1843O, plain 4, large date	200.00	465.00
1844	235.00	850.00
1844C	800.00	2,600.00
1844D	850.00	2,400.00
1845	190.00	350.00
1845D	950.00	2,600.00
1845O	550.00	2,300.00
1846	200.00	500.00
1846C	850.00	3,500.00
1846D	900.00	2,150.00
1846O	190.00	400.00
1847	150.00	370.00
1847C	950.00	2,200.00
1847D	990.00	2,250.00
1847O	160.00	410.00
1848	315.00	850.00
1848, CAL.	13,500.00	30,000.00

Quarter eagles with CAL over the eagle were struck with gold shipped to the Dept. of War by the governor of California.

	VF	XF
1848C	900.00	2,250.00
1848D	2,200.00	2,500.00
1849	200.00	475.00
1849C	900.00	2,250.00
1849D	950.00	2,500.00
1850	160.00	275.00
1850C	900.00	2,250.00
1850D	950.00	2,500.00
1850O	170.00	450.00
1851	150.00	220.00
1851C	990.00	2,300.00
1851D	1,100.00	2,600.00
1851O	150.00	250.00
1852	150.00	210.00
1852C	900.00	2,150.00
1852D	950.00	2,900.00
1852O	160.00	300.00
1853	135.00	225.00

1852D 2-1/2-Dollar Gold Piece with Coronet (No Motto)

1859 2-1/2-Dollar Gold Piece with Coronet (No Motto)

	VF	XF		VF	XF
1853D	990.00	3,500.00	1857S	160.00	340.00
1854	150.00	210.00	1858	150.00	250.00
1854C	700.00	2,000.00	1858C	900.00	2,100.00
1854D	1,800.00	5,000.00	1859	150.00	265.00
1854O	150.00	240.00	1859D	1,100.00	3,400.00
1854S	70,000.00	125,000.00	1859S	200.00	900.00
1855	150.00	230.00	1860	150.00	265.00
1855C	900.00	3,500.00	1860C	950.00	2,300.00
1855D	2,000.00	7,500.00	1860S	170.00	675.00
1856	150.00	210.00	1861	150.00	210.00
1856C	750.00	2,500.00	1861S	200.00	1,000.00
1856D	4,000.00	12,500.00	1862, 2 over 1	475.00	2,000.00
1856O	180.00	750.00	1862	160.00	300.00
1856S	160.00	380.00	1862S	500.00	2,100.00
1857	150.00	210.00	1863, proof only	—	60,000.00
1857D	900.00	3,000.00	1863S	300.00	1,500.00
1857O	155.00	350.00	1864	2,500.00	10,000.00

	VF	XF		VF	XF
1865	2,400.00	8,200.00	1879S	155.00	275.00
1865S	160.00	650.00	1880	170.00	335.00
1866	650.00	3,500.00	1881	850.00	3,200.00
1866S	180.00	650.00	1882	160.00	290.00
1867	190.00	800.00	1883	175.00	400.00
1867S	170.00	675.00	1884	175.00	400.00
1868	170.00	400.00	1885	400.00	1,800.00
1868S	150.00	350.00	1886	170.00	270.00
1869	170.00	450.00	1887	175.00	245.00
1869S	160.00	440.00	1888	160.00	240.00
1870	165.00	420.00	1889	155.00	230.00
1870S	155.00	400.00	1890	170.00	240.00
1871	160.00	325.00	1891	165.00	215.00
1871S	150.00	300.00	1892	170.00	250.00
1872	210.00	725.00	1893	165.00	215.00
1872S	155.00	425.00	1894	170.00	230.00
1873, closed 3	150.00	220.00	1895	150.00	225.00
1873, open 3	150.00	200.00	1896	150.00	225.00
1873S	160.00	425.00	1897	150.00	215.00
1874	170.00	380.00	1898	150.00	215.00
1875	1,950.00	5,000.00	1899	150.00	215.00
1875S	150.00	300.00	1900	150.00	240.00
1876	170.00	650.00	1901	150.00	215.00
1876S	170.00	525.00	1902	150.00	215.00
1877	275.00	700.00	1903	150.00	215.00
1877S	150.00	215.00	1904	150.00	215.00
1878	150.00	215.00	1905	150.00	215.00
1878S	150.00	215.00	1906	150.00	215.00
1879	150.00	215.00	1907	150.00	215.00

1911D 2-1/2-Dollar Gold Piece with Indian Head

INDIAN HEAD TYPE

	VF	AU		VF	AU
1908	175.00	230.00	1914D	175.00	230.00
1909	175.00	230.00	1915	175.00	230.00
1910	175.00	230.00	1925D	175.00	230.00
1911	175.00	230.00	1926	175.00	230.00
1911D	2,500.00	5,200.00	1927	175.00	230.00
1912	175.00	230.00	1928	175.00	230.00
1913	175.00	230.00	1929	180.00	250.00
1914	175.00	260.00			

THREE-DOLLAR GOLD PIECES

The 1851 law which lowered the rate for first class mail from five cents to three cents also authorized a three-cent coin with which to purchase the new stamps. The prevailing thought at the time continued, and in 1853, another law authorized a three-dollar gold piece, which could be used to conveniently purchase entire sheets of stamps, as well as be exchanged for 100 of the small silver trimes. Popularly called a portrait of an Indian princess, the design is more specifically that of Liberty wearing a feathered headdress, and was also used on the Type III gold dollars of 1856. It was never particularly popular, with most years outside the 1850s struck in insignificant quantities. Mintages became almost ceremonial until striking was finally suspended in 1889.

In its day it was popularly used as jewelry, so collectors must be very careful to inspect coins for traces of solder. Look for irregularities in the reeding or discoloration near the edge. Cleaning is both a problem and a hint to other flaws such as mount marks.

★ ★ COUNTERFEIT ALERT ★ ★

1877 exists by altering genuine coins of other dates. Struck counterfeits exist of virtually every date in this series.

1884 Three-Dollar Gold Piece

	VF	XF
1854	850.00	1,150.00
1854D	9,000.00	15,000.00
1854O	1,500.00	2,700.00
1855	900.00	1,150.00
1855S	1,200.00	2,500.00
1856	880.00	1,150.00
1856S	900.00	1,600.00
1857	900.00	1,150.00
1857S	950.00	2,800.00
1858	950.00	2,000.00
1859	900.00	1,800.00
1860	900.00	1,600.00
1860S	950.00	2,350.00
1861	950.00	1,600.00
1862	950.00	1,850.00
1863	900.00	1,500.00
1864	950.00	1,550.00
1865	1,500.00	3,000.00
1866	970.00	1,500.00
1867	950.00	1,500.00
1868	750.00	1,200.00
1869	1,150.00	1,600.00

	VF	XF
1870	1,000.00	1,500.00
1870S		*unique*
1871	1,000.00	1,500.00
1872	950.00	1,800.00
1873, closed 3	4,000.00	6,000.00
1873, open 3, *proof only*	—	65,000.00
1874	800.00	1,300.00
1875, *proof only*	—	175,000.00
1876	6,000.00	10,000.00
1877	1,500.00	3,300.00
1878	800.00	1,300.00
1879	800.00	1,300.00
1880	850.00	1,800.00
1881	1,800.00	3,000.00
1882	925.00	1,400.00
1883	1,000.00	1,600.00
1884	1,250.00	1,800.00
1885	1,200.00	1,500.00
1886	1,200.00	1,800.00
1887	900.00	1,300.00
1888	950.00	1,500.00
1889	925.00	1,300.00

FIVE-DOLLAR GOLD PIECES

The first American gold coin to be struck was the half eagle, or $5 gold piece in 1795. Its first obverse features a bust of Liberty wearing a tall conical cap traditionally, but inaccurately, referred to by numismatists as a turban. Originally, this was paired with a reverse design featuring a skinny eagle similar to that on the first dollars, but instead of standing within a wreath it is seen holding one above its head. As with the other denominations, this was replaced by a plumper heraldic eagle bearing a shield on its chest, which later was featured on all denominations other than copper. The original bust by Robert Scott was replaced in 1807 by one designed by John Reich, and was wearing a smaller cap. A reverse eagle similar, but more realistic, was paired with the new obverse. While the design and net gold content did not change for almost 30 years, the coin's diameter was at first increased and then reduced.

Through most of its history until the 1830s, the half eagle was plagued by mass meltings, being undervalued relative to its gold content, particularly by European standards. In 1834, this was remedied by reducing the coin's gold content. This was indicated to the public by the removal of the motto over the eagle on the reverse, and by a new capless Liberty head, the "Classic Head" by William Kneass. The final Coronet-type Liberty head design was a rendition by Christian Gobrecht, which continued in use from 1839 to 1908, the motto replaced over the eagle in 1866.

In 1908, as part of the same coin design beautification program which later introduced the Walking Liberty half dollar and St. Gaudens double eagle, sculptor Bela Lyon Pratt was asked to prepare new designs for the quarter and half eagle in secret under the authority of President Theodore Roosevelt. His work showed the bust of an Indian chief on the obverse and an eagle with closed wings on the reverse. It was both controversial and innovative in that it bore its design in relief, but recessed below the surface of the coin. While some criticized it both for aesthetic reasons and for fear of it spreading germs in dirt trapped in the recesses, it proved to be a very successful method of shielding the design from wear.

★ ★ COUNTERFEIT ALERT ★ ★

1811, 1815 (altered), 1841O (probable), 1852C, 1854S (altered), 1858, 1870CC (altered), 1875, 1877 (altered), 1885, 1885S, 1887 Proof (altered), 1892, 1892O (altered), 1906S, 1907D, 1908 (Liberty), 1908D, 1909 Matte Proof, 1909D, 1909O, 1910D, 1914D, 1914S, and 1915D (all counterfeit), among others. Be cautious of false C mintmarks altered by cutting down an authentic O mintmark. Beware of traces of solder on earlier coins from use as jewelry. Look for interruption in the pattern of edge reeding. Be cautious of cleaned coins. This is harder to detect on gold, which usually does not tone naturally.

1795 Five-Dollar Gold Piece with Turban Bust and Small Eagle

TURBAN BUST/SMALL EAGLE

	F	VF		F	VF
1795	14,500.00	20,000.00	1797, 16 stars	18,000.00	22,500.00
1796, 6 over 5	16,000.00	21,500.00	1798	100,000.00	190,000.00
1797, 15 stars	23,500.00	30,000.00			

1803/2 Five-Dollar Gold Piece with Turban Bust and Heraldic Eagle

TURBAN BUST/HERALDIC EAGLE

	F	VF
1795	10,000.00	17,500.00
1797, 7 over 5	14,000.00	21,500.00
1797, 16 star obv.	—	unique
1798, small 8	4,000.00	7,000.00
1798, large 8, 13 star rev.	3,300.00	4,000.00
1798, large 8, 14 star rev.	3,500.00	5,000.00
1799	3,500.00	5,000.00
1800	3,500.00	5,000.00

	F	VF
1802, 2 over 1	3,500.00	5,000.00
1803, 3 over 2	3,500.00	5,000.00
1804, small 8	3,500.00	5,000.00
1804, small 8 over large 8	3,500.00	5,000.00
1805	3,500.00	5,000.00
1806, pointed 6	3,600.00	5,000.00
1806, round 6	3,500.00	5,000.00
1807	3,500.00	5,100.00

1810 Five-Dollar Gold Piece with Capped Bust (small date, tall 5)

CAPPED BUST TYPE

	F	VF
1807	2,500.00	3,500.00
1808, 8 over 7	3,200.00	4,300.00
1808	2,500.00	3,500.00
1809, 9 over 8	2,500.00	3,500.00

	F	VF
1810, small date, small 5	12,000.00	23,000.00
1810, small date, tall 5	2,500.00	3,800.00

	F	VF
1810, large date, small 5	15,000.00	30,000.00
1810, large date, large 5	2,800.00	3,500.00
1811, small 5	2,800.00	3,500.00
1811, tall 5	2,700.00	3,500.00
1812	2,500.00	3,500.00
1813	2,700.00	3,600.00
1814, 4 over 3	2,700.00	3,600.00
1815	EF	85,000.00
1818	3,000.00	4,000.00
1818, STATES OF	3,000.00	3,800.00
1818, 5D over 50	3,000.00	4,000.00
1819	13,500.00	26,500.00

	F	VF
1819, 5D over 50	—	25,000.00
1820, curved-base	23,500.00	4,800.00
1820, square-base	23,500.00	4,800.00
1821	14,000.00	24,000.00
1822	1,500,000.00	—
1823	3,000.00	4,000.00
1824	6,000.00	12,000.00
1825, 5 over 1	6,100.00	14,000.00
1825, 5 over 4	*only two known*	
1826	5,000.00	8,500.00
1827	6,000.00	10,000.00
1828, 8 over 7	20,000.00	32,000.00
1828	8,000.00	17,500.00
1829	—*extremely rare*	

1834 Five-Dollar Gold Piece with Classic
Head and Crosslet 4 (No Motto)

CAPPED BUST/REDUCED DIAMETER

	F	VF
1829	40,000.00	65,000.00
1830	16,500.00	20,000.00
1831	16,500.00	20,000.00
1832, 12 stars	*only six known*	
1832, 13 stars	16,500.00	20,000.00
1833	16,500.00	20,000.00
1834, plain 4	16,500.00	20,000.00
1834, crosslet 4	16,500.00	20,000.00

CLASSIC HEAD (NO MOTTO)

	VF	XF
1834, plain 4	500.00	840.00
1834, crosslet 4	2,000.00	3,600.00
1835	500.00	850.00
1836	500.00	840.00
1837	500.00	870.00
1838	500.00	840.00
1838C	2,850.00	4,850.00
1838D	2,450.00	4,500.00

1841 Five-Dollar Gold Piece with Coronet (No Motto)

CORONET TYPE (NO MOTTO)

	VF	XF
1839	275.00	480.00
1839C	2,300.00	3,000.00
1839D	2,200.00	3,200.00
1840	275.00	360.00
1840C	2,300.00	3,100.00
1840D	2,300.00	3,200.00
1840O	375.00	900.00
1841	400.00	950.00
1841C	1,800.00	2,400.00
1841D	1,800.00	2,400.00
1841O	—	..two known
1842, small letters	345.00	1,100.00
1842, large letters	750.00	2,000.00
1842C, small date	9,950.00	23,000.00
1842C, large date	1,800.00	2,300.00
1842D, small letters	2,000.00	2,350.00
1842D, large letters	2,500.00	6,700.00
1842O	1,000.00	3,400.00

	VF	XF
1843	275.00	330.00
1843C	1,850.00	2,500.00
1843D	1,950.00	2,600.00
1843O, small letters	660.00	1,800.00
1843O, large letters	265.00	1,175.00
1844	275.00	330.00
1844C	1,900.00	3,300.00
1844D	1,950.00	2,400.00
1844O	275.00	375.00
1845	275.00	280.00
1845D	1,900.00	2,400.00
1845O	415.00	800.00
1846, small date	275.00	330.00
1846	275.00	330.00
1846C	1,900.00	3,000.00
1846D	1,800.00	2,500.00
1846O	375.00	1,000.00
1847	275.00	280.00

	VF	XF
1847C	1,850.00	2,500.00
1847D	2,000.00	2,500.00
1847O	2,400.00	6,700.00
1848	275.00	285.00
1848C	1,900.00	2,250.00
1848D	2,000.00	2,350.00
1849	275.00	280.00
1849C	1,900.00	2,400.00
1849D	2,000.00	2,575.00
1850	300.00	625.00
1850C	1,850.00	2,300.00
1850D	1,950.00	2,500.00
1851	275.00	280.00
1851C	1,900.00	2,350.00
1851D	1,950.00	2,400.00
1851O	590.00	1,450.00
1852	275.00	280.00
1852C	1,900.00	2,450.00
1852D	2,000.00	2,450.00
1853	275.00	280.00
1853C	1,950.00	2,350.00
1853D	2,000.00	2,500.00
1854	275.00	280.00
1854C	1,900.00	2,300.00
1854D	1,875.00	2,200.00
1854O	300.00	525.00
1854S	—	extremely rare
1855	275.00	280.00
1855C	1,950.00	2,300.00
1855D	1,950.00	2,400.00
1855O	675.00	2,100.00
1855S	390.00	1,000.00
1856	275.00	280.00
1856C	1,875.00	2,400.00
1856D	1,950.00	26,900.00
1856O	650.00	1,600.00
1856S	300.00	700.00
1857	275.00	280.00
1857C	1,900.00	2,500.00
1857D	2,000.00	2,600.00
1857O	640.00	1,400.00
1857S	300.00	700.00
1858	275.00	550.00
1858C	1,900.00	2,350.00
1858D	2,000.00	2,450.00
1858S	825.00	2,400.00
1859	325.00	625.00
1859C	1,900.00	2,450.00
1859D	2,150.00	2,600.00
1859S	1,800.00	4,100.00
1860	280.00	575.00
1860C	2,100.00	2,950.00
1860D	1,900.00	2,600.00
1860S	1,100.00	2,100.00
1861	275.00	280.00
1861C	2,400.00	4,000.00
1861D	4,800.00	7,000.00
1861S	1,000.00	4,500.00
1862	800.00	1,850.00
1862S	3,000.00	6,000.00
1863	1,200.00	3,700.00
1863S	1,450.00	4,100.00
1864	650.00	1,850.00
1864S	6,000.00	16,000.00
1865	1,400.00	4,000.00
1865S	1,400.00	2,400.00
1866S	1,700.00	4,000.00

1866 Five-Dollar Gold Piece with Coronet and Motto

CORONET TYPE (WITH MOTTO)

	VF	XF		VF	XF
1866	800.00	1,600.00	1876	1,100.00	2,500.00
1866S	900.00	2,600.00	1876CC	1,500.00	5,000.00
1867	500.00	1,500.00	1876S	2,000.00	3,600.00
1867S	1,400.00	2,900.00	1877	900.00	2,700.00
1868	650.00	1,000.00	1877CC	1,000.00	3,300.00
1868S	400.00	1,550.00	1877S	400.00	650.00
1869	925.00	1,900.00	1878	265.00	280.00
1869S	500.00	1,750.00	1878CC	3,100.00	9,500.00
1870	800.00	1,950.00	1878S	265.00	280.00
1870CC	5,250.00	15,000.00	1879	265.00	280.00
1870S	950.00	2,600.00	1879CC	575.00	1,500.00
1871	875.00	1,700.00	1879S	265.00	280.00
1871CC	1,200.00	3,000.00	1880	265.00	280.00
1871S	500.00	1,000.00	1880CC	425.00	800.00
1872	675.00	1,700.00	1880S	265.00	280.00
1872CC	1,200.00	5,000.00	1881, 1 over 0	330.00	600.00
1872S	460.00	800.00	1881	265.00	280.00
1873, closed 3	265.00	280.00	1881CC	550.00	1,500.00
1873, open 3	265.00	280.00	1881S	265.00	280.00
1873CC	2,600.00	12,500.00	1882	265.00	280.00
1873S	525.00	1,400.00	1882CC	420.00	625.00
1874	660.00	1,450.00	1882S	265.00	280.00
1874CC	850.00	1,750.00	1883	265.00	280.00
1874S	650.00	2,100.00	1883CC	460.00	1,100.00
1875	34,000.00	45,000.00	1883S	265.00	280.00
1875CC	1,400.00	4,500.00	1884	265.00	280.00
1875S	715.00	2,250.00	1884CC	575.00	985.00

1899 Five-Dollar Gold Piece with Coronet and Motto

	VF	XF		VF	XF
1884S	265.00	280.00	1896	265.00	280.00
1885	265.00	280.00	1896S	265.00	285.00
1885S	265.00	280.00	1897	265.00	280.00
1886	265.00	280.00	1897S	265.00	280.00
1886S	265.00	280.00	1898	265.00	280.00
1887, *proof only*	—	60,000.00	1898S	265.00	280.00
1887S	265.00	280.00	1899	265.00	280.00
1888	265.00	280.00	1899S	265.00	280.00
1888S	265.00	280.00	1900	265.00	280.00
1889	350.00	440.00	1900S	265.00	280.00
1890	390.00	475.00	1901	265.00	280.00
1890CC	350.00	460.00	1901S, 1 over 0	265.00	280.00
1891	265.00	280.00	1901S	265.00	280.00
1891CC	350.00	450.00	1902	265.00	280.00
1892	265.00	280.00	1902S	265.00	280.00
1892CC	350.00	450.00	1903	265.00	280.00
1892O	520.00	990.00	1903S	265.00	280.00
1892S	265.00	280.00	1904	265.00	280.00
1893	265.00	280.00	1904S	270.00	295.00
1893CC	350.00	465.00	1905	265.00	280.00
1893O	265.00	315.00	1905S	265.00	280.00
1893S	265.00	280.00	1906	265.00	280.00
1894	265.00	280.00	1906D	265.00	280.00
1894O	265.00	360.00	1906S	265.00	280.00
1894S	265.00	375.00	1907	265.00	280.00
1895	265.00	280.00	1907D	265.00	280.00
1895S	265.00	295.00	1908	265.00	280.00

1908 Five-Dollar Gold Piece with Indian Head

INDIAN HEAD TYPE

	VF	XF		VF	XF
1908	330.00	360.00	1911S	330.00	360.00
1908D	330.00	360.00	1912	330.00	360.00
1908S	380.00	425.00	1912S	330.00	360.00
1909	330.00	360.00	1913	330.00	360.00
1909D	330.00	360.00	1913S	340.00	370.00
1909O	2,100.00	3,500.00	1914	330.00	360.00
1909S	330.00	360.00	1914D	335.00	365.00
1910	330.00	360.00	1914S	340.00	375.00
1910D	330.00	360.00	1915	330.00	360.00
1910S	330.00	360.00	1915S	340.00	400.00
1911	330.00	360.00	1916S	330.00	360.00
1911D	475.00	540.00	1929	5,000.00	10,000.00

10-DOLLAR GOLD PIECES

Among the first two American gold coins to be struck was the eagle or $10 gold piece in 1795, and it was George Washington himself who received the first example. Its first obverse features a bust of Liberty by Robert Scot, wearing a tall conical cap traditionally, but inaccurately, referred to by numismatists as a turban. Originally, this was paired with a reverse design featuring a skinny eagle similar to that on the first silver dollars, but instead of standing within a wreath, it is seen holding one above its head. As with the other denominations, this was replaced by a plumper heraldic eagle bearing a shield on its chest, which later was featured on all denominations other than copper.

All these early eagles were struck on a primitive screw press with hand engraved dies, no two of which were identical. Many will show evidence of adjustment marks, a scraping of metal from the blank before striking to prevent the coin from being overweight. While not desirable, they are not considered damage, as they are part of the manufacturing process.

The initial issue of 1795-1804 was plagued by mass meltings and wholesale export, being undervalued relative to its gold content, particularly by European standards. As a result, its coinage was completely suspended for more than 30 years. It was reintroduced in 1838 on the reduced gold standard adopted in 1834 to prevent these abuses. The new gold eagle featured a Liberty head wearing a coronet, Christian Gobrecht's interpretation of a painting of Venus by Benjamin West. A new, more realistic reverse eagle still wore a heraldic shield. This design continued in use until 1907, the motto replaced over the eagle in 1866.

In 1908, as part of the same coin design beautification trend which later introduced the Walking Liberty half dollar and Mercury dime, noted sculptor Augustus St. Gaudens was asked to prepare new designs for the eagle and double eagle by President Theodore Roosevelt. His work showed the head of Liberty wearing an Indian warbonnet, the headdress being added to St. Gauden's head originally designed as Victory at the president's instruction. The reverse featured a very proud eagle with closed wings.

As Roosevelt believed the use of the motto "In God We Trust" on coinage to be a debased use of the divine name, it was omitted from the initial issues. This upset Congress so much that a law was enacted that restored it in 1908.

★ ★ COUNTERFEIT ALERT ★ ★

1799, 1858 (altered), 1889 (altered from Ps), 1901S, 1906D, 1906S, 1907, 1908 with Motto Proof, 1908S, 1909 Matte Proof, 1909S, 1910 Proof, 1910S, 1911 Proof, 1911D, 1911S, 1912S, 1913, 1913S, 1914S, 1915S, 1916S, 1926, 1932, 1933, among others especially 1870 to 1933. Be cautious of false C mintmarks altered by cutting down an authentic O mintmark. Beware of traces of solder on earlier coins from use as jewelry. Look for interruption in the pattern of edge reeding. Be cautious of cleaned coins. This is harder to detect on gold which usually does not tone naturally.

1795 10-Dollar Gold Piece with Turban Bust and Small Eagle (13 leaves)

TURBAN BUST/SMALL EAGLE

	F	VF
1795, 9 leaves below eagle	35,000.00	50,000.00
1795, 13 leaves	24,000.00	32,000.00

	F	VF
1796	26,000.00	37,000.00
1797	30,000.00	45,000.00

1799 10-Dollar Gold Piece with Turban Bust and Heraldic Eagle

TURBAN BUST/HERALDIC EAGLE

	F	VF
1797	11,500.00	15,500.00
1798/9,7 9 stars l., 4 r.	18,000.00	28,000.00
1798/97, 7 stars l., 6 r.	35,000.00	55,000.00

	F	VF
1799	9,500.00	11,000.00
1800	9,500.00	11,000.00
1801	9,500.00	11,000.00
1803	9,500.00	11,000.00
1804	13,500.00	19,500.00

1849O 10-Dollar Gold Piece with Coronet (No Motto)

CORONET TYPE (NO MOTTO)

	VF	XF
1838	1,200.00	2,900.00
1839, large letters	1,150.00	1,950.00
1839, small letters	1,600.00	3,500.00
1840	515.00	650.00
1841	515.00	550.00
1841O	3,200.00	6,000.00
1842, small date	515.00	600.00
1842, large date	515.00	535.00
1842O	515.00	530.00
1843	515.00	535.00
1843O	515.00	535.00
1844	1,350.00	2,900.00
1844O	515.00	535.00
1845	600.00	775.00
1845O	515.00	750.00
1846	625.00	950.00
1846O	515.00	800.00
1847	515.00	535.00
1847O	515.00	535.00
1848	515.00	535.00
1848O	575.00	1,100.00
1849	515.00	535.00
1849O	710.00	2,100.00
1850, large date	515.00	535.00
1850, small date	515.00	535.00
1850O	515.00	875.00
1851	515.00	535.00
1851O	515.00	535.00
1852	515.00	535.00
1852O	650.00	1,100.00
1853, 3 over 2	600.00	800.00
1853	515.00	535.00
1853O	515.00	535.00
1854	515.00	535.00
1854O, small date	515.00	675.00
1854O, large date	515.00	865.00
1854S	515.00	535.00
1855	515.00	535.00
1855O	600.00	1,200.00
1855S	1,500.00	2,500.00
1856	515.00	535.00
1856O	725.00	1,250.00
1856S	515.00	535.00
1857	520.00	850.00
1857O	995.00	1,850.00
1857S	515.00	995.00
1858	5,200.00	8,200.00
1858O	515.00	750.00
1858S	1,600.00	3,100.00
1859	515.00	750.00
1859O	4,000.00	8,500.00
1859S	2,000.00	5,000.00
1860	515.00	775.00
1860O	575.00	1,250.00
1860S	3,250.00	6,100.00
1861	515.00	535.00
1861S	1,600.00	2,950.00
1862	550.00	1,200.00
1862S	2,000.00	3,000.00
1863	3,850.00	9,950.00

1862S 10-Dollar Gold Piece with Coronet (No Motto)

	VF	XF
1863S	1,700.00	3,500.00
1864	1,700.00	4,500.00
1864S	5,100.00	13,000.00
1865	1,950.00	3,600.00

	VF	XF
1865S	5,800.00	12,000.00
1865S, 865 over inverted 186	3,100.00	6,500.00
1866S	2,800.00	3,800.00

1873CC 10-Dollar Gold Piece with Coronet and Motto

CORONET TYPE (WITH MOTTO)

	VF	XF
1866	850.00	1,800.00
1866S	1,550.00	4,000.00
1867	1,500.00	2,600.00
1867S	2,100.00	6,000.00
1868	550.00	800.00
1868S	1,300.00	2,600.00
1869	1,600.00	2,950.00
1869S	1,600.00	2,700.00
1870	850.00	1,475.00
1870CC	9,990.00	30,000.00
1870S	1,300.00	2,950.00
1871	1,600.00	3,000.00

	VF	XF
1871CC	2,600.00	5,950.00
1871S	1,300.00	1,750.00
1872	2,400.00	3,600.00
1872CC	3,100.00	11,000.00
1872S	550.00	950.00
1873	4,500.00	9,500.00
1873CC	5,000.00	10,000.00
1873S	950.00	2,400.00
1874	515.00	530.00
1874CC	950.00	3,100.00
1874S	1,150.00	3,250.00
1875	40,000.00	59,000.00

1882O 10-Dollar Gold Piece with Coronet and Motto

	VF	XF		VF	XF
1875CC	4,200.00	11,000.00	1885S	515.00	530.00
1876	3,500.00	6,300.00	1886	515.00	530.00
1876CC	2,500.00	8,000.00	1886S	515.00	530.00
1876S	1,450.00	1,900.00	1887	515.00	530.00
1877	2,600.00	5,700.00	1887S	515.00	530.00
1877CC	2,600.00	6,750.00	1888	515.00	530.00
1877S	530.00	850.00	1888O	515.00	530.00
1878	515.00	530.00	1888S	515.00	530.00
1878CC	4,000.00	10,000.00	1889	575.00	675.00
1878S	515.00	615.00	1889S	515.00	530.00
1879	515.00	530.00	1890	515.00	530.00
1879CC	9,500.00	15,000.00	1890CC	535.00	575.00
1879O	2,300.00	3,800.00	1891	515.00	530.00
1879S	515.00	530.00	1891CC	535.00	600.00
1880	515.00	530.00	1892	515.00	530.00
1880CC	590.00	900.00	1892CC	535.00	600.00
1880O	505.00	780.00	1892O	515.00	530.00
1880S	515.00	530.00	1892S	515.00	530.00
1881	515.00	530.00	1893	515.00	530.00
1881CC	525.00	800.00	1893CC	565.00	900.00
1881O	525.00	800.00	1893O	515.00	530.00
1881S	515.00	530.00	1893S	515.00	530.00
1882	515.00	530.00	1894	515.00	530.00
1882CC	950.00	1,300.00	1894O	515.00	530.00
1882O	515.00	575.00	1894S	515.00	540.00
1882S	515.00	530.00	1895	515.00	530.00
1883	515.00	530.00	1895O	515.00	530.00
1883CC	575.00	915.00	1895S	515.00	530.00
1883O	3,300.00	7,200.00	1896	515.00	530.00
1883S	515.00	530.00	1896S	515.00	530.00
1884	515.00	530.00	1897	515.00	530.00
1884CC	600.00	1,100.00	1897O	515.00	530.00
1884S	515.00	530.00	1897S	515.00	530.00
1885	515.00	530.00	1898	515.00	530.00

1901 10-Dollar Gold Piece with Coronet and Motto

	VF	XF		VF	XF
1898S	515.00	530.00	1903S	515.00	530.00
1899	515.00	530.00	1904	515.00	530.00
1899O	515.00	530.00	1904O	515.00	530.00
1899S	515.00	530.00	1905	515.00	530.00
1900	515.00	530.00	1905S	515.00	530.00
1900S	515.00	530.00	1906	515.00	530.00
1901	515.00	530.00	1906D	515.00	530.00
1901O	515.00	530.00	1906O	515.00	530.00
1901S	515.00	530.00	1906S	515.00	530.00
1902	515.00	530.00	1907	515.00	530.00
1902S	515.00	530.00	1907D	515.00	530.00
1903	515.00	530.00	1907S	515.00	530.00
1903O	515.00	530.00			

1907 10-Dollar Gold Piece with Indian Head and No Motto

INDIAN HEAD/NO MOTTO

	VF	XF		VF	XF
1907, wire rim, periods.	—	15,000.00	1907, no periods	580.00	620.00
1907, rounded rim, periods	39,000.00	—	1908	580.00	630.00
			1908D	580.00	620.00

1913 10-Dollar Gold Piece with Indian Head and Motto

INDIAN HEAD/WITH MOTTO

	VF	XF		VF	XF
1908	580.00	620.00	1913	580.00	620.00
1908D	580.00	620.00	1913S	600.00	660.00
1908S	580.00	620.00	1914	580.00	620.00
1909	580.00	620.00	1914D	580.00	620.00
1909D	580.00	620.00	1914S	580.00	620.00
1909S	580.00	620.00	1915	580.00	620.00
1910	580.00	620.00	1915S	625.00	750.00
1910D	580.00	620.00	1916S	580.00	620.00
1910S	580.00	620.00	1920S	7,800.00	11,000.00
1911	580.00	620.00	1926	580.00	620.00
1911D	625.00	725.00	1930S	5,500.00	8,000.00
1911S	600.00	650.00	1932	580.00	620.00
1912	580.00	620.00	1933	*MS-60*	200,000.00
1912S	580.00	620.00			

FIRST SPOUSE TEN-DOLLAR GOLD PIECES

Issued in conjunction with the circulating Presidential dollars, this series of $10 gold pieces depicts the First Lady of each presidency. The Jefferson, Jackson, and Van Buren administration's coin depicts Liberty, as there was no First Lady during their years in office.

★ ★ COUNTERFEIT ALERT ★ ★
None reported to date.

2007W 10-Dollar Gold Piece
Martha Washington

2007W 10-Dollar Gold Piece
Abigail Adams

MARTHA WASHINGTON

	MS-63	PF
2007W	600.00	600.00

ABIGAIL ADAMS

	MS-63	PF
2007W	600.00	600.00

2007W 10-Dollar Gold Piece Liberty
(Jefferson)

2007W 10-Dollar Gold Piece
Dolley Madison

LIBERTY (JEFFERSON)

	MS-63	PF
2007W	600.00	600.00

DOLLEY MADISON

	MS-63	PF
2007W	600.00	600.00

2008W 10-Dollar Gold Piece
Elizabeth Monroe

2008W 10-Dollar Gold Piece
Louisa Adams

ELIZABETH MONROE

	MS-63	PF
2008W	600.00	600.00

LOUISA ADAMS

	MS-63	PF
2008W	600.00	600.00

2008W 10-Dollar Gold Piece Liberty
(Jackson)

2008W 10-Dollar Gold Piece Liberty
(Van Buren)

LIBERTY (JACKSON)

	MS-63	PF
2008W	600.00	600.00

LIBERTY (VAN BUREN)

	MS-63	PF
2008W	600.00	600.00

20-DOLLAR GOLD PIECES

The California Gold Rush of the 1840s resulted in large quantities of bullion being received at the Mint for coinage. Partially to make this massive coinage more expedient and partially because of the obvious convenience of using fewer coins for large international payments, the bill proposing the introduction of gold dollars was amended to include a large $20 gold piece called a "double eagle." James B. Longacre engraved a bust of Liberty wearing a coronet similar to, but of much more refined style, than the one in use on smaller gold since 1838. A facing heraldic eagle with a circlet of stars and a radiant arc above graced the reverse, the two motto ribbons at its sides suggesting the denomination of two eagles.

This design continued in use until 1907, the motto being placed within the circlet over the eagle in 1866. Two other minor modifications were attempted. The first (1861), called the Paquet reverse, is a subtle rearrangement of details, and for technical reasons was abandoned almost immediately. The other was the replacement in 1877 of the abbreviation D. with the word "dollars."

In 1908, as part of the same coin design beautification trend which later introduced the Walking Liberty half dollar and Mercury dime, noted sculptor Augustus St. Gaudens was asked by President Theodore Roosevelt to prepare new designs for the double eagle and eagle. His work showed a full figure of Liberty, holding a torch and olive branch, striding towards the viewer. It was very much inspired by Hellenistic sculpture, as correspondence between the two men clearly confirms. The reverse featured an eagle in mid-flight with a rising sun and rays in the background.

As Roosevelt believed the use of the motto "In God We Trust" on coinage to be a debased use of the divine name, it was omitted from the initial issues. This upset Congress so much that a law was enacted replacing it in 1908. To avoid public confusion the date was changed from Roman numerals to Arabic ones, and because the initial design was of such high relief that it took three strikes by the dies, its relief was lowered as well.

Both the Liberty type and the Saint Gaudens type are often found with heavy bag marks due to their soft metal and heavy weight. Examples virtually free from bagging command a substantial premium.

★ ★ COUNTERFEIT ALERT ★ ★

1879, 1879O, 1881 (altered), 1882 (altered), 1887 (altered), 1891, 1894, 1897S, 1898S, 1899S, 1900, 1900S, 1901S, 1903, 1903S, 1904, 1904S, 1906, 1906S, MCMVII, 1907 (Saint-Gaudens), 1908, 1909,

1910D, 1910S, 1911D, 1914D, 1914S, 1915, 1916S, 1919, 1920, 1921, 1922, 1923, 1924, 1925, 1926, 1927, 1927D (altered), 1928, 1929, among others, especially 1870 to 1932. This series generally has been extensively counterfeited, be cautious. Beware of traces of solder on earlier coins from use as jewelry. Look for interruption in the pattern of edge reeding. Be cautious of cleaned coins. This is harder to detect on gold, which usually does not tone naturally.

1850 20-Dollar Gold Piece with Liberty Head (Type I)

LIBERTY HEAD—TYPE I

	VF	XF
1849		unique
1850	1,045.00	1,325.00
1850O	1,100.00	2,400.00
1851	1,045.00	1,090.00
1851O	1,050.00	1,400.00
1852	1,045.00	1,090.00
1852O	1,200.00	1,400.00
1853, 3 over 2	1,050.00	1,300.00
1853	1,045.00	1,090.00
1853O	1,045.00	2,200.00
1854	1,045.00	1,090.00
1854O	90,000.00	180,000.00
1854S	1,045.00	1,090.00
1855	1,045.00	1,090.00
1855O	3,200.00	9,500.00
1855S	1,045.00	1,090.00
1856	1,045.00	1,090.00
1856O	90,000.00	150,000.00
1856S	1,045.00	1,090.00
1857	1,045.00	1,090.00
1857O	1,300.00	2,600.00
1857S	1,045.00	1,090.00
1858	1,045.00	1,090.00
1858O	1,800.00	2,750.00
1858S	1,045.00	1,090.00
1859	1,150.00	2,450.00
1859O	4,700.00	9,000.00
1859S	1,045.00	1,090.00
1860	1,045.00	1,090.00
1860O	4,550.00	9,000.00
1860S	1,045.00	1,090.00
1861	1,045.00	1,090.00
1861O	3,300.00	6,700.00

Most of these were struck by Louisiana and the Confederacy after withdrawal from the Union.

	VF	XF
1861S	1,045.00	1,090.00
1861, Paquet rev.	Proof-67	660,000.00
1861S, Paquet rev.	20,000.00	38,000.00
1862	1,050.00	2,000.00
1862S	1,045.00	1,500.00
1863	1,045.00	1,500.00
1863S	1,045.00	1,400.00
1864	1,045.00	1,100.00
1864S	1,045.00	1,090.00
1865	1,045.00	1,090.00
1865S	1,045.00	1,090.00
1866S	3,000.00	11,000.00

1869S 20-Dollar Gold Piece with Liberty Head and Motto (Type II)

LIBERTY HEAD (WITH MOTTO)—
TYPE II

	VF	XF		VF	XF
1866	1,045.00	1,100.00	1872CC	2,400.00	3,300.00
1866S	1,045.00	1,085.00	1872S	1,045.00	1,085.00
1867	1,045.00	1,085.00	1873, closed 3	1,045.00	1,085.00
1867S	1,045.00	1,085.00	1873, open 3	1,045.00	1,085.00
1868	1,050.00	1,200.00	1873CC	2,250.00	3,500.00
1868S	1,045.00	1,085.00	1873S	1,045.00	1,085.00
1869	1,045.00	1,085.00	1874	1,045.00	1,085.00
1869S	1,045.00	1,085.00	1874CC	2,400.00	3,300.00
1870	1,045.00	1,200.00	1874S	1,045.00	1,085.00
1870CC	150,000.00	200,000.00	1875	1,045.00	1,085.00
1870S	1,045.00	1,085.00	1875CC	1,300.00	1,500.00
1871	1,045.00	1,085.00	1875S	1,045.00	1,090.00
1871CC	8,000.00	15,000.00	1876	1,045.00	1,090.00
1871S	1,045.00	1,085.00	1876CC	1,300.00	1,500.00
1872	1,045.00	1,085.00	1876S	1,045.00	1,090.00

1877 20-Dollar Gold Piece with Liberty Head (Type III)

1903 20-Dollar Gold Piece with Liberty Head (Type III)

LIBERTY HEAD—TYPE III

	VF	XF		VF	XF
1877	1,040.00	1,080.00	1889CC	1,500.00	1,600.00
1877CC	1,500.00	1,900.00	1889S	1,040.00	1,080.00
1877S	1,040.00	1,080.00	1890	1,040.00	1,080.00
1878	1,040.00	1,080.00	1890CC	1,250.00	1,600.00
1878CC	2,200.00	3,300.00	1890S	1,040.00	1,080.00
1878S	1,040.00	1,080.00	1891	4,000.00	6,500.00
1879	1,040.00	1,080.00	1891CC	3,800.00	9,000.00
1879CC	2,500.00	4,000.00	1891S	1,040.00	1,080.00
1879O	9,500.00	15,000.00	1892	1,300.00	2,100.00
1879S	1,040.00	1,080.00	1892CC	1,350.00	1,650.00
1880	1,040.00	1,080.00	1892S	1,040.00	1,080.00
1880S	1,040.00	1,080.00	1893	1,040.00	1,080.00
1881	5,000.00	8,000.00	1893CC	1,650.00	1,950.00
1881S	1,040.00	1,080.00	1893S	1,040.00	1,080.00
1882	8,000.00	23,500.00	1894	1,040.00	1,080.00
1882CC	1,200.00	1,500.00	1894S	1,040.00	1,080.00
1882S	1,040.00	1,080.00	1895	1,040.00	1,080.00
1883, *proof only*		100,000.00	1895S	1,040.00	1,080.00
1883CC	1,350.00	1,600.00	1896	1,040.00	1,080.00
1883S	1,040.00	1,080.00	1896S	1,040.00	1,080.00
1884, *proof only*		100,000.00	1897	1,040.00	1,080.00
1884CC	1,250.00	1,550.00	1897S	1,040.00	1,080.00
1884S	1,040.00	1,080.00	1898	1,040.00	1,080.00
1885	7,000.00	9,800.00	1898S	1,040.00	1,080.00
1885CC	2,900.00	4,000.00	1899	1,040.00	1,080.00
1885S	1,040.00	1,080.00	1899S	1,040.00	1,080.00
1886	12,000.00	18,500.00	1900	1,040.00	1,080.00
1887, *proof only*		60,000.00	1900S	1,040.00	1,080.00
1887S	1,040.00	1,080.00	1901	1,040.00	1,080.00
1888	1,040.00	1,080.00	1901S	1,040.00	1,080.00
1888S	1,040.00	1,080.00	1902	1,040.00	1,080.00
1889	1,040.00	1,080.00	1902S	1,040.00	1,080.00

	VF	XF
1903	1,040.00	1,080.00
1903S	1,040.00	1,080.00
1904	1,040.00	1,080.00
1904S	1,040.00	1,080.00
1905	1,040.00	1,080.00
1905S	1,040.00	1,080.00

	VF	XF
1906	1,040.00	1,080.00
1906D	1,040.00	1,080.00
1906S	1,040.00	1,080.00
1907	1,040.00	1,080.00
1907D	1,040.00	1,080.00
1907S	1,040.00	1,080.00

1907 High Relief 20-Dollar Saint Gaudens Gold Piece with No Motto

SAINT-GAUDENS/NO MOTTO

	VF	XF
1907, high relief, wire rim	7,250.00	9,750.00
1907, high relief, flat rim	7,500.00	10,250.00

	VF	XF
1907, Arabic numerals	1,040.00	1,090.00
1908	1,040.00	1,090.00
1908D	1,040.00	1,090.00

SAINT-GAUDENS/WITH MOTTO

	VF	XF
1908	1,040.00	1,080.00
1908D	1,040.00	1,080.00
1908S	1,450.00	2,200.00
1909/8	1,040.00	1,080.00
1909	1,040.00	1,080.00
1909D	1,040.00	1,080.00
1909S	1,040.00	1,080.00
1910	1,040.00	1,080.00
1910D	1,040.00	1,080.00
1910S	1,040.00	1,080.00
1911	1,040.00	1,080.00
1911D	1,040.00	1,080.00
1911S	1,040.00	1,080.00

	VF	XF
1912	1,040.00	1,080.00
1913	1,040.00	1,080.00
1913D	1,040.00	1,080.00
1913S	1,060.00	1,150.00
1914	1,040.00	1,080.00
1914D	1,040.00	1,080.00
1914S	1,040.00	1,080.00
1915	1,040.00	1,080.00
1915S	1,040.00	1,080.00
1916S	1,040.00	1,080.00
1920	1,040.00	1,080.00
1920S	12,500.00	18,000.00
1921	20,000.00	30,000.00

1909 20-Dollar Saint Gaudens Gold Piece with Motto

	VF	XF
1922	1,040.00	1,080.00
1922S	1,040.00	1,080.00
1923	1,040.00	1,080.00
1923D	1,040.00	1,080.00
1924	1,040.00	1,080.00
1924D	1,200.00	1,550.00
1924S	1,200.00	1,600.00
1925	1,040.00	1,080.00
1925D	1,600.00	2,200.00
1925S	1,400.00	2,000.00
1926	1,040.00	1,080.00
1926D	7,500.00	11,000.00

	VF	XF
1926S	1,100.00	1,550.00
1927	1,040.00	1,080.00
1927D	—	350,000.00
1927S	5,000.00	8,500.00
1928	1,040.00	1,080.00
1929	5,750.00	9,000.00
1930S	15,000.00	27,500.00
1931	9,900.00	14,500.00
1931D	9,000.00	12,500.00
1932	8,200.00	15,000.00
1933	*MS-65*	9,000,000.00

United States Paper Money

Introduction

Before the Civil War, there was no such thing as United States government paper money. During the Revolutionary War the states and the Continental Congress printed so much paper money to finance their expenses that its value evaporated, and it became nearly worthless. As a result, when the Constitution was written it contained the words "No state shall...make anything but gold and silver coin a tender in payment of debts. (1§10)." Because of this, the government avoided issuing paper money until the Civil War, and even then it was issued under limited circumstances. The first type of paper money, Demand Notes, even bore interest.

Most of the paper money issued by the United States over the following century was redeemable for gold or silver. There are many different kinds of American paper money, as the following sections will show. Their names, usually found at the top of the note as a heading, and often the colors of their seals indicate the law that authorized their issue and the nature of their backing.

Almost all United States paper currency bears a date, but this is not necessarily the year it was actually printed. It was the year of the act authorizing the series or the year the series went into production. The signature combinations on banknotes can often be used to date them.

Originally paper money was larger than today. Until 1928 they were about 7-1/2 x 3-1/8 inches. Beginning with the series of 1928 (released 1929) they have been 6-1/8 x 2-5/8 inches. The fractional notes of the Civil War were smaller than current notes, but varied in size.

Grading Paper Money

State of preservation is as important for paper money as it is for coins. Paper money is primarily graded to describe the amount of wear. Other factors can influence value though. Many of the terms used to describe the grades of paper money are the same as for coins. Of course the physical nature of paper requires a whole different set of definitions. They are briefly described here.

Crisp Uncirculated (CU)—This note is as pristine as when issued. It is literally crisp, with sharply pointed corners. It must have absolutely no folds, tears, or edge rounding. It can have no stains or staple holes either.

Extremely Fine (XF)—This is a particularly nice note with only the slightest sign of wear. It will still be crisp to the touch. Slight rounding of the corner points is possible, but no significant folds or creases. No tears, stains or staple holes at all.

A convenient method of detecting creases in a note is to hold the note pointed at a narrow light source and look at it from an acute angle, though not directly in the direction of the light.

Very Fine (VF)—This is a nice clean note with obvious, but moderate, signs of wear. Creases which break the ink will be visible, but generally only one in each direction, and neither crease too deep. Its corner points will be dull. While not limp, it will have only some of the crispness of better grade notes. No significant stains are visible.

Fine (F)—This is a worn, but not worn-out note. It has no crispness left. It will have heavy creases, but none that threaten the structural integrity of the note. Its edges may not be perfectly smooth, but are not irregularly worn. Trivial ink marks and smudges are acceptable.

Very Good (VG)—This note is worn and limp. It has serious deep creases. The edges are worn and not even. Some ink marks or smudges are visible. Tiny tears may be present, but no parts missing. Small staple or pin holes are acceptable.

Good (G)—This condition is not considered collectible for most purposes. Only the rarest of notes in this grade could find a home with most collectors. It is usually limp, heavily creased, stained, ripped, and pinned or stapled. Some of the creases will permit spots of light to shine through the note at their intersections.

Handling and Treatment of Paper Money

The most important thing to know about handling currency is to **never fold paper money**. This instantaneously reduces its value. When in doubt as to whether a note has value or not, place it flat in a book until you can consult a numismatist or coin dealer. Do not carry an interesting note around in your wallet. When handling a note remember that its most fragile parts are its corners. Never touch them. Also, never repair a tear in a note with tape. The tape usually is a greater detriment to the note's value than the tear. Attempts to clean a note are also likely to cause damage.

Detecting Counterfeit Paper Money

Detecting counterfeit notes is not as difficult or as mysterious a business as many presume. Also, many of the methods used by merchants are so inefficiently used as to be of no value.

First, it must be realized that almost since its beginning, United States paper money has been printed not on paper, but on cloth. It is part cotton and part linen with some silk. The silk is in the form of minute red and blue threads which dive in and out of the surface of the note. A color copier may be able to reproduce the colors of these tiny threads, but it cannot reproduce the texture of them entering and leaving the surface of the note. Use a magnifying glass. Another key to detecting counterfeits is crispness of the ink in the design. Images and lines should be sharp and distinct.

Minimal effort looking for these clues can catch most circulating counterfeits. Most counterfeit bills passed in circulation are accepted not because the counterfeits are deceptive, but because little or no effort is put into looking to see if they are real at all. This is entertainingly illustrated by the occasional news story about the cashier who accepts a spoof note in payment.

In recent years, Federal Reserve Notes have incorporated many new counterfeit detection devices. These are fully described in that section.

Real notes have been used occasionally to create counterfeits. A counterfeiter will take the value numbers from the corners of a note and glue them to a note of a lower face value. Such notes will often feel too thick or irregular at the corners. More importantly, such a criminal is presuming the recipients will pay virtually no attention to the notes they are accepting. Such counterfeits can be detected by even the quickest comparison with a real note.

Certain practices are designed to take an authentic note and make it appear to be in a better grade of preservation than it is. These include ironing a note to make it look less worn, and expertly gluing tears. Hold your note up to a light. Light will pass through the glue differently than through normal currency.

When choosing a rare currency dealer it is good to make sure that they have the skills to know a note is real, and the ethics to accept it back if it is not. Of course the same principles apply as mentioned above in choosing a coin dealer. There are specialized organizations that enforce codes of ethics. Two of the largest are the International Banknote Society (IBNS) and the Professional Currency Dealers Association (PCDA). These insignia in advertising indicate that the dealer is a member.

10-Dollar Treasury Note, Series 1890

DEMAND NOTES

The demand notes of 1861 were the very first regular paper money issued by the United States. They were put into circulation under the emergency circumstances of the Civil War. The bad experiences of the overproduction of paper money during the Revolutionary War were still remembered, so limits were set on the uses of these notes. They differed from modern currency mostly in that they were not properly legal tender, but rather were "receivable in payment for all public dues." That is to say they were not good for "all debts public and private," and not by initial obligation for any private debts at all. One could use them to pay taxes, but did not have to accept them otherwise. Later a law was passed requiring their acceptance. Their name Demand Note derives from another phrase on their face, "The United States promises to pay to the bearer on demand."

On the other hand, there were limits as to how they could be redeemed. These notes were issued at five cities and could only be redeemed by the assistant treasurers in the individual note's specific city of issue. Designs were uniform from city to city. The $5 note shows at left the statue of Columbia from the Capitol building, a portrait of Alexander Hamilton right. The $10 shows Lincoln, then in office, left, an eagle centered, and an allegorical figure of Art right. The $20 depicts Liberty holding a sword and shield.

The nickname "green back" for paper money began with these notes, which have a distinctive green back. The privately issued paper money circulating until then had blank backs.

There are two major varieties of these, resulting from the government being ill prepared for the practical reality of hand signing millions of notes. The original intent was that clerks would be able to sign them "N. for the" Register of the Treasury and "N. for the" Treasurer of the United States. The time it took to sign the words "for the" millions of times quickly became excessive, so the notes were modified so the words were printed on instead. The earlier varieties are worth more than the prices listed here. High-grade notes in this series are very rare.

★ ★ COUNTERFEIT ALERT ★ ★

Examine detail, check to make sure notes are hand signed, and use reasonable caution.

	G	VG			G	VG
$5 Boston	450.00	3,500.00		$10 Boston	950.00	3,700.00
$5 Cincinnati	rare	—		$10 Cincinnati	rare	—
$5 New York	450.00	3,500.00		$10 New York	950.00	3,400.00
$5 Philadelphia	450.00	3,500.00		$10 Philadelphia	950.00	3,400.00
$5 St. Louis	1,000.00	rare		$10 St. Louis	3,000.00	8,000.00
				$20 Boston	12,500.00	22,000.00
				$20 Cincinnati	—	rare
				$20 New York	8,500.00	22,000.00
				$20 Philadelphia	8,500.00	22,000.00

Philadelphia Five-Dollar Demand Note, Series 1861

TREASURY NOTES

These notes, designated "Treasury Notes" by the titles on their face inscriptions, are also called "Coin Notes." This was because, according to law, the Secretary of the Treasury was instructed to redeem these notes in coin, either gold or silver, at his choosing. Interestingly, they were not actually backed by coin at all, but rather by silver bullion.

This series was of very short duration, being issued only in 1890 and 1891. Both years have the same face designs, generally of military heroes. The original reverse designs featured the values spelled out in large letters. For 1891, they were redesigned to allow more blank space. The ornamentation of the two 0s in 100 on the reverse of the $100 notes is reminiscent of the pattern on the skin of a watermelon, hence they are known by the collecting community as "watermelon notes."

★ ★ COUNTERFEIT ALERT ★ ★

Examine detail, silk threads in paper, and use reasonable caution.

Two-Dollar Treasury Note, Series 1890

	F	XF
$1 1890		
Edwin M. Stanton.	650.00	2,500.00
$1 1891 same	350.00	650.00
$2 1890 Gen. James D.		
McPherson	1,000.00	6,500.00
$2 1891 same	500.00	2,000.00
$5 1890 Gen. George H.		
Thomas	600.00	3,000.00
$5 1891 same	350.00	750.00
$10 1890 Gen. Philip H.		
Sheridan	1,500.00	3,500.00
$10 1891 same	950.00	1,900.00
$20 1890 John		
Marshall	3,400.00	7,500.00
$20 1891 same	3,000.00	7,400.00

10-Dollar Treasury Note, Series 1890

	F	XF
$50 1891 William H. Seward	40,000.00	120,000.00
$100 1890 Adm. David G. Farragut	70,000.00	150,000.00

	F	XF
$100 1891 same	70,000.00	150,000.00
$1000 1890 Gen. George Meade	rare	—
$1000 1891 same	rare	—

NATIONAL BANK NOTES

National bank notes are a hybrid of government issued and private paper money. The notes, titled "National Currency" on their face, were issued by individual private banks, but printed by the U.S. government. Not every bank could issue them, only "national banks." To qualify each bank had to meet certain criteria, which included keeping a predetermined value of U.S. government bonds on deposit with the United States Treasurer. In exchange for this commitment, the notes issued by any bank were considered legal tender of the United States and were good anywhere United States currency was good. The Treasury would stand behind these notes.

Designs did not vary from bank to bank, but they used those types designated by the Treasury. The face of each note would indicate the issuing bank's name (usually including the word "national") and its charter number. Many earlier notes would also show the coat of arms of its native state.

Each of over 1,300 issuing banks was assigned a charter number. There were three periods under which banks could apply for a 20-year charter. The first period was 1863-1882. Those banks securing their charters during this period could issue notes of the first charter reverse design as late as 1902. Those banks receiving their charters from 1882 to 1902, the second period, issued notes of a new type back designed for second charter banks. These were actually printed 1882 to 1922. Those banks receiving their charters during the third period of authorization, 1902 to 1922, issued yet a third series of different designs from 1902 to 1929. It is seen that this system determines the design (and often apparent "date") on a note not by when it was issued, but by when the issuing bank first received its charter. Hence, different designs of a National Bank Note could be issued at the same time with different dates! A very confusing situation.

Just like all other currency, nationals were reduced in size in 1929. Type 1 notes (1929-33) have the charter number on the face twice. Type 2 notes (1933-35) have it four times. When, in May 1935, the Treasury recalled many of the bonds which the national banks were using as security, National Bank Notes ceased to be issued.

Nationals have been among the most sought-after notes in a generally active U.S. paper money market. Not all nationals of a given type are worth the same, as certain states and cities are more popularly collected than others. Also, some banks ordered very small quantities of notes. The following values are for the most common and least expensive banks issuing that type of note. Large-size nationals from Alaska, Arizona, Hawaii, Idaho, Indian Territory, Mississippi, Nevada, New Mexico, Puerto Rico, and South Dakota are automatically worth more. The same is true for small-size nationals from Alaska, Arizona, Hawaii, Idaho, Montana, Nevada, and Wyoming.

★ ★ COUNTERFEIT ALERT ★ ★

Examine detail, silk threads in paper, and use reasonable caution.

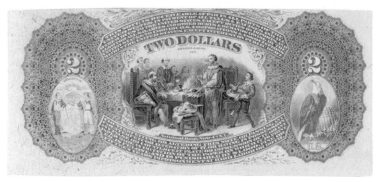

Two-Dollar National Bank Note, First Charter, Series 1875

FIRST CHARTER (1863-1875)

	VG	VF
$1 Allegory of Concord/Pilgrims landing, ND		
(original series)	950.00	2,000.00
same, 1875	950.00	2,000.00

	VG	VF
$2 Lazy 2/Sir Walter Raleigh, ND		
(original series)	3,000.00	5,000.00
same, 1875	3,000.00	5,000.00

	VG	VF
$5 Columbus sighting land/landing of Columbus, ND (original series)	1,300.00	2,600.00
same, 1875	1,300.00	2,600.00

	VG	VF
$10 Franklin experimenting with lightning/DeSoto, ND		
(original series)	1,900.00	3,600.00
same, 1875	1,900.00	3,600.00

10-Dollar National Bank Note, First Charter, Series 1875

	VG	VF
$20 Battle of Lexington/baptism of Pocahontas, ND (original series)	2,700.00	4,500.00
same, 1875	2,700.00	4,250.00
$50 Washington Crossing Delaware and at prayer/Pilgrims, ND (original series)	15,000.00	20,000.00

	VG	VF
$100 Battle of Lake Erie/signing of the Declaration of Independence, ND (original series)	17,000.00	23,000.00
$500	—	unique
$1,000	—	unique

Five-Dollar National Bank Note, Brown Back
with Charter Numbers, Second Charter, Series 1872

Five-Dollar National Bank Note,
with Large *1882* 1908*, Second Charter, Series 1882

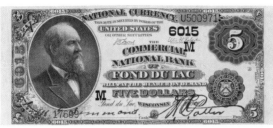

Five-Dollar National Bank Note, Value Back
with Large Spelled-Out Value, Second Charter, Series 1882

SECOND CHARTER/SERIES OF 1882
"Brown Backs" with charter number

	VG	VF
$5 James Garfield	700.00	1,000.00
$10 as 1st charter	1,000.00	1,700.00
$20 as 1st charter	1,200.00	2,000.00
$50 as 1st charter	5,500.00	7,000.00
$100 as 1st charter	6,700.00	8,000.00

SECOND CHARTER/SERIES OF 1882
"Value Backs" large spelled-out value

	VG	VF
$5 James Garfield	750.00	1,150.00
$10 as 1st charter	900.00	1,200.00
$20 as 1st charter	1,200.00	1,750.00
$50 as 1st charter	45,000.00	70,000.00
$100 as 2nd series	90,000.00	*extremely rare*

SECOND CHARTER/SERIES OF 1882
*"Date Backs" with large "1882*1908"*

	VG	VF
$5 James Garfield	650.00	850.00
$10 as 1st charter	870.00	1,250.00
$20 as 1st charter	1,200.00	1,700.00
$50 as 1st charter	5,500.00	6,500.00
$100 as 1st charter	7,500.00	8,200.00

50-Dollar National Bank Note, Third Charter, Series 1902

50-Dollar National Bank Note, Third Charter, Series 1902

Five-Dollar Small-Size, Type 2 National Bank Note
(serial number and bank number in brown), Series 1929

THIRD CHARTER/SERIES OF 1902
Red Treasury Seal on face

	VG	VF
$5 Benjamin Harrison/Pilgrims landing	700.00	1,100.00
$10 William McKinley/Columbia between ships	1,000.00	1,250.00
$20 Hugh McCulloch/Columbia and Capitol	1,200.00	4,800.00
$50 John Sherman/train	5,700.00	6,500.00
$100 John Knox/eagle on shield	7,500.00	11,000.00

THIRD CHARTER/SERIES OF 1902
Blue Treasury Seal, "1902-1908" on back

	VG	VF
$5 as red seals	200.00	350.00
$10 as red seals	200.00	400.00
$20 as red seals	200.00	400.00
$50 as red seals	1,300.00	2,000.00
$100 as red seals	1,200.00	2,700.00

THIRD CHARTER/SERIES OF 1902
Blue Treasury Seal, "Plain Backs" without dates

	VG	VF
$5 as red seals	160.00	300.00
$10 as red seals	160.00	300.00
$20 as red seals	160.00	350.00
$50 as red seals	1,200.00	1,800.00
$100 as red seals	1,100.00	2,700.00

50-Dollar Small-Size National Bank Note, Type 2, Series 1929

THIRD CHARTER/SERIES OF 1929
Brown Treasury Seal, Small-Size Notes

	VG	VF		VG	VF
$5 Type 1	60.00	100.00	$20 Type 2	80.00	150.00
$5 Type 2	70.00	120.00	$50 Type 1	300.00	450.00
$10 Type 1	75.00	120.00	$50 Type 2	350.00	650.00
$10 Type 2	90.00	175.00	$100 Type 1	375.00	600.00
$20 Type 1	75.00	120.00	$100 Type 2	375.00	650.00

NATIONAL GOLD BANK NOTES

These notes were like National Bank Notes, but they were specifically redeemable in gold coin. They were a co-operative issue of the individual National Gold Bank, which held the obligation, and the U.S. Treasury. Every bank had to be a regular national bank as well, and meet all the reserve requirements. But these national banks were authorized by the Treasury to issue notes redeemable in gold.

The reason for their issue from 1870-75 was to relieve the banks in California of the daily handling of massive quantities of gold coin. All but one of the banks authorized to issue these was located in California. The very design of these notes reflects their backing by gold. Their paper is a golden yellow, and the reverse bears an array of United States gold coins of every denomination. Their remarkably fine engraving gives the coins a very realistic appearance. Because other types of notes were not very popular in California, these notes got some very hard use, and today are rare in all but worn-out condition.

★ ★ COUNTERFEIT ALERT ★ ★

Examine detail, and look for correct yellow paper, which occasionally may tone down. Use reasonable caution.

	G	F
$5 Columbus sighting land	**1,700.00**	**6,000.00**
$10 Franklin experimenting with lightning	**2,500.00**	**15,000.00**
$20 Battle of Lexington	**8,000.00**	**15,000.00**

	G	F
$50 Washington crossing Delaware and at prayer	**15,000.00**	**rare**
$100 Battle of Lake Erie	**38,000.00**	**rare**

UNITED STATES NOTES

While most of these notes will carry the title "United States Note" at the top or bottom of their face, some earlier ones actually say "Treasury Note" instead. The very first notes omit both. They are, however, the same according to the legislation that authorized them. They are the longest lasting kind of American paper money, issued from 1862 until 1966. There are a great many different designs, of which the "Bison Ten" is the most famous and most popular. Just like all other currency, United States Notes were reduced in size with the "series of 1928" in 1929. Small-size notes are occasionally found in circulation today, and are characterized by a red Treasury seal. The latter, when worn, are not generally considered collectible.

This series includes popular "star" notes. These are notes with part of the serial number replaced by a star. They were printed to replace notes accidentally destroyed in manufacturing. These were introduced first on $20 notes in 1880 and eventually descended to $1 notes by 1917. They usually are worth more.

★ ★ COUNTERFEIT ALERT ★ ★

Examine detail, silk threads in paper, and use reasonable caution. In addition to counterfeits made to fool collectors, early circulation counterfeits of the 1863 $50, 1869 $50, and 1863 $100 exist.

Two-Dollar Large-Size United States Note, Series 1875

	F	XF
$1 1862 Salmon P. Chase, red seal	600.00	1,250.00
$1 1869 Washington, Columbus scene/US intertwined	600.00	1,500.00
$1 1874-1917 same/large X	95.00	140.00
$1 1923 Washington bust	185.00	450.00
$2 1862 Alexander Hamilton double circle	775.00	2,200.00
$2 1869 Jefferson and Capitol/II•2•TWO	950.00	3,500.00
$2 1874-1917 same/II•TWO omitted	140.00	225.00
$5 1862 Statue of Columbia l., Alexander Hamilton r.	465.00	1,250.00
$5 1863 same, different obligation on back	500.00	875.00

Five-Dollar Large-Size United States Note, Series 1869

	F	XF
$5 1869 Jackson l., pioneer family center/ circle with 5	600.00	1,750.00
$5 1875-1907 same, red seal/ circle with concentric pattern	190.00	350.00

10-Dollar Large-Size United States Note, Series 1862

	F	XF
$5 1880 same, brown seal	435.00	850.00
$10 1862 Lincoln and allegory of Art	1,375.00	3,000.00
$10 1862-63 same, different obligation on back	1,375.00	3,000.00

10-Dollar Large-Size United States Note, Series 1901

	F	XF
$10 1869 Daniel Webster and Pocahontas/inscription centered	750.00	3,500.00
$10 1875-80 same/inscription at right	500.00	1,400.00
$10 1880 same, brown seal	535.00	1,100.00
$10 1901 Bison/Columbia standing between pillars	750.00	2,200.00
$10 1923 Andrew Jackson/value	1,300.00	5,000.00
$20 1862 Liberty with sword and shield	2,000.00	16,000.00
$20 1862-63 same, different obligation on back	2,000.00	6,800.00
$20 1869 Alexander Hamilton l.,Victory standing r.	2,900.00	9,900.00
$20 1875-80 same/no inscription at center	400.00	1,200.00
$20 1880 same, brown seal	1,000.00	2,500.00

	F	XF
$50 1862 Alexander Hamilton	30,000.00	43,000.00
$50 1862-63 same, different obligation on back	12,500.00	300,000.00
$50 1869 Peace and Henry Clay	32,000.00	50,000.00
$50 1874-80 Franklin and Columbia	3,000.00	9,500.00
$50 same, brown seal	4,500.00	30,000.00
$100 1862 Eagle	30,000.00	50,000.00
$100 1862-63 same, different obligation on back	30,000.00	65,000.00
$100 1869 Lincoln and allegory of Architecture/inscription centered	17,500.00	50,000.00
$100 1875-80 same, inscription at left	9,000.00	17,500.00
$100 1880, same, brown seal	9,000.00	30,000.00
$500 1862 Albert Gallatin **rare**	—	

One-Dollar Small-Size United States Note, Red Seal, Series 1928

	F	XF
$500 1862-63 same, different obligation on back.......... **rare** .... —		
$500 1869 John Quincy Adams .... **rare** .... —		
$500 1874-80 Gen. Joseph Mansfield .... **rare** .... —		
$500 1880 same, brown seal .... **rare** .... —		
$1,000 1862 Robert Morris .... **rare** .... —		
$1,000 1862-63 same, different obligation on back.......... **rare** .... —		
$1,000 1869 Columbus and DeWitt Clinton/inscription centered......... **rare** .... —		
$1,000 1878-80 same, inscription at left .... **rare** .... —		
$1,000 1880 same, brown seal .... **rare** .... —		

SMALL SIZE NOTES—RED SEAL

$1 1928 Washington/ONE
$2 1928-63A Jefferson/Monticello
$5 1928-63 Lincoln/Lincoln Memorial
$100 1966-66A Franklin/Indep. Hall

	F	XF
$1 1928	75.00	250.00
$2 1928	18.00	50.00
$2 1928A	40.00	100.00
$2 1928B	90.00	450.00
$2 1928C	15.00	27.00
$2 1928D	15.00	25.00
$2 1928E	15.00	30.00
$2 1928F	15.00	25.00
$2 1928G	13.50	24.00

Five-Dollar Small-Size United States Note, Red Seal, Series 1928

	CU
$2 1953	18.00
$2 1953A	11.00
$2 1953B	10.00
$2 1953C	9.00
$2 1963	8.00
$2 1963A	9.00

	F	XF
$5 1928	15.00	28.00
$5 1928A	15.00	45.00
$5 1928B	14.00	28.00
$5 1928C	13.00	25.00

	XF	CU
$5 1928D	35.00	75.00
$5 1928E	13.00	25.00
$5 1928F	10.00	25.00
$5 1953	9.00	15.00
$5 1953A	7.00	18.00
$5 1953B	7.00	15.00
$5 1953C	7.50	25.00
$5 1963	7.00	15.00
$100 1966	220.00	350.00
$100 1966A	365.00	900.00

GOLD CERTIFICATES

As the title on these notes implies, these were notes both backed by reserves in gold coin and payable to the bearer in that coin. The first Gold Certificates were issued in 1865-75, but were used for transactions between banks. Notes of this period not listed are not known to have survived. The issue of 1882 was the first for general circulation. Again the issues of 1888-89 were only of $5,000 and $10,000 and not widely circulated. Regular issues were again placed in circulation in 1905-07. This series includes a $20 note so beautifully colored with black, red and gold ink on white gold-tinted paper that it has come to have the nickname of "Technicolor." Those of the series of 1913-28 are the most common Gold Certificates.

Like all other notes of the 1928 series, these gold certificates were printed on the reduced size paper still used today. These are distinguished from other kinds of small-size notes by a gold Treasury seal. The final issues, those of 1934, were again just for bank transactions. The government recalled these notes from general circulation in 1933 when it withdrew gold coinage. Today, they are perfectly legal to own but far scarcer due to this earlier destruction.

★ ★ COUNTERFEIT ALERT ★ ★

Examine detail on 1882 and later silk threads in paper, and use reasonable caution.

20-Dollar Gold Certificate, Series 1882

FIRST ISSUE—1863

$20 Eagle on shield . . . — . . **500,000.00**
$100 Eagle on shield . . — *extremely rare*

SECOND ISSUE—1870-71

No notes known to have survived.

THIRD ISSUE—1870S

$100 Thomas H. Benton— *extremely rare*

FOURTH ISSUE—SERIES OF 1882

	F	XF
$20 James Garfield	**950.00**	**5,000.00**
$50 Silas Wright. . . .	**1,750.00**	**5,000.00**
$100 Thomas Benton	**1,150.00**	**2,800.00**
$500 Abraham Lincoln	**10,500.00**	**25,000.00**
$1,000 Alexander Hamilton	*rare*	—
$5,000 James Madison .	*rare*	—
$10,000 Andrew Jackson	*rare*	—

FIFTH ISSUE—SERIES OF 1888

	F	XF
$5000 James Madison. . . .	—	*rare*
$10,000 Andrew Jackson .	—	*rare*

20-Dollar Gold Certificate, Series 1922

SIXTH ISSUE—SERIES OF 1900

	F	XF
$10,000 Jackson		
cut cancelled		**3,000.00**

SEVENTH ISSUE— SERIES OF 1905-07

	F	XF
$10 Michael Hillegas	250.00	**675.00**
$20 Washington 1905 "technicolor note"	**2,300.00**	**8,000.00**
$20 Washington 1906	300.00	**800.00**

EIGHTH ISSUE—SERIES OF 1907

	F	XF
$1,000 Alexander Hamilton	**12,000.00**	**38,000.00**

NINTH ISSUE—SERIES OF 1913

	F	XF
$50 Ulysses S. Grant	900.00	**3,000.00**

TENTH ISSUE—SERIES OF 1922

	F	XF
$10 Michael Hillegas	250.00	**650.00**
$20 Washington	**300.00**	**700.00**
$50 Ulysses S. Grant	850.00	**2,500.00**
$100 Thomas Benton	**950.00**	**3,500.00**
$500 Abraham Lincoln	*rare*	—
$1,000 Alexander Hamilton	*rare*	—

10-Dollar Small-Size Gold Certificate, Series 1928

SMALL SIZE—SERIES OF 1928

	F	XF
$10 Alex. Hamilton	125.00	350.00
$20 Andrew Jackson	125.00	300.00
$50 Ulysses S. Grant	400.00	1,200.00
$100 Ben. Franklin	650.00	2,000.00

	F	XF
$500 W. McKinley	5,000.00	12,000.00
$1,000 G. Cleveland	8,500.00	22,000.00
$5,000 James Madison	rare	—

SILVER CERTIFICATES

On the same day, Feb. 28, 1878, as the authorization by Congress for the striking of millions of silver dollars, it also passed legislation authorizing Silver Certificates. This is not pure coincidence. Silver Certificates were not simply backed up by silver bullion, but represented actual silver dollars held by the Treasury. The issue of this series of notes was what in part made it necessary to strike millions of Morgan dollars, and was ultimately prompted by heavy lobbying by the silver mining industry.

Some of the most famous or beautiful banknotes issued by the U.S. are Silver Certificates. These include the "Educational" $1, $2, and $5 of 1896, the "Onepapa Five," and the "Porthole Five." The name "Onepapa Five" is a misnomer. It depicts Chief Running Antelope of the Uncpapa Sioux, but because the name sounded so unfamiliar to early collectors it was quickly mispronounced "Chief One Papa."

Just like all other currency, Silver Certificates were reduced in size with the "series of 1928" in 1929.

During World War II there was fear that supplies of U.S. currency would fall into enemy hands if certain territories were overrun. The response to this was to make sure that notes distributed in these territories had distinguishing features that permitted their identification and repudiation if captured. Those Silver Certificates issued to troops in North Africa were printed with a yellow Treasury seal instead of a blue one. Notes distributed in Hawaii feature the word "HAWAII" overprinted very large on the back.

The motto "In God We Trust" was added to the one-dollar note for the 1935 G and H and all 1957 series. They continued to be issued until the 1957B series in 1963. Small-size silver certificates are occasionally found in circulation today and are easily recognized by a blue Treasury seal. These notes when worn are not generally considered collectible, but do have some novelty value. They have not been able to be redeemable for silver dollars since 1968.

This series includes popular "star" notes. These are notes with part of the serial number replaced by a star. They are printed to replace notes accidentally destroyed in the manufacturing process. These were introduced first in 1899. They often, but not always, are worth somewhat more.

★ ★ COUNTERFEIT ALERT ★ ★

Examine detail of silk threads in paper and use reasonable caution. Circulating counterfeits exist for this series and are slightly less dangerous.

One-Dollar Large-Size Silver Certificate, Series 1896

	F	XF
$1 1886 Martha Washington/inscription in oval	400.00	850.00
$1 1891 same/inscription in rosette	500.00	950.00
$1 1896 History instructing youth/ George and Martha Washington	450.00	1,100.00

	F	XF
$1 1899 Eagle	150.00	275.00
$1 1923 Washington	45.00	75.00
$2 1886 Gen. Winfield Scott Hancock	700.00	1,750.00

Two-Dollar Large-Size Silver Certificate, Series 1896

	F	XF
$2 1891 Sen. William Windom	650.00	2,500.00
$2 1896 Science Presenting Steam and Electricity to Commerce and Industry/Fulton and Morse	1,000.00	4,500.00

	F	XF
$2 1899 Washington, Mechanics and Agriculture	265.00	900.00

Five-Dollar Large-Size Silver Certificate, Series 1899

	F	XF
$5 1886 Ulysses S. Grant/Morgan silver dollars	1,250.00	4,600.00
$5 1891 same/ inscription	800.00	2,000.00
$5 1896 Winged Electricity lighting the World	2,500.00	6,300.00

	F	XF
$5 1899 Chief "Onepapa"	650.00	1,900.00
$5 1923 Lincoln in porthole-like frame/great seal	1,700.00	2,750.00

10-Dollar Large-Size Silver Certificate, Series 1891

	F	XF
$10 1878-80 Robert Morris/S I L V E R	1,700.00	8,500.00
$10 1886 Thomas Hendricks in tombstone-like frame	1,250.00	4,000.00
$10 1891-1908 same/UNITED STATES in oval	750.00	1,850.00
$20 1878-80 Capt. StephenDecatur/ S I L V E R	3,700.00	12,500.00
$20 1886 Daniel Manning/double diamond	4,000.00	13,000.00
$20 1891 same/double circle	1,500.00	3,750.00

	F	XF
$50 1878-80 Edward Everett/ S I L V E R	9,900.00	35,000.00
$50 1891 same/inscription in center	2,500.00	4,500.00
$100 1878-80 James Monroe/ S I L V E R	16,000.00	45,000.00
$100 1891 same/inscription in center	8,000.00	44,000.00
$500 1878-80 Sen. Charles Sumner/ S I L V E R	rare	—
$1,000 1878-80 William Marcy	rare	—
$1,000 1891 Columbia and Marcy	rare	—

One-Dollar Small-Size Silver Certificate, Blue Seal, Series 1928

SMALL SIZE NOTES—BLUE SEAL

$1 1928-28E Washington/ONE
$1 1934-57B Washington/Great Seal
$5 1934-53C Lincoln/Lincoln Memorial
$10 1933-53B Hamilton/Treasury

	F	XF
$1 1928	26.00	45.00
$1 1928A	26.00	45.00
$1 1928B	26.00	45.00
$1 1928C	120.00	400.00
$1 1928D	45.00	200.00
$1 1928E	600.00	1,150.00
$1 1934	40.00	55.00
$1 1935	6.00	10.00
$1 1935A	4.00	5.00
$1 1935A, HAWAII	40.00	70.00
$1 1935A, yellow seal	45.00	75.00
$1 1935A, red R	75.00	130.00
$1 1935A, red S	75.00	150.00
$1 1935B	4.00	5.00
$1 1935C	3.00	4.00
$1 1935D	3.00	4.00

	XF	CU
$1 1935E	—	9.00
$1 1935F	9.00	—
$1 1935G,	9.50	—
same with motto	6.00	30.00
$1 1935H	10.00	—
$1 1957	9.00	—
$1 1957A	9.00	—
$1 1957B	9.00	—
$5 1934	18.00	35.00
$5 1934A	15.00	25.00
$5 1934A, yellow seal	95.00	220.00
$5 1934B	12.00	30.00
$5 1934C	10.00	23.00
$5 1934D	10.00	23.00
$5 1953	21.00	—
$5 1953A	20.00	—
$5 1953B	20.00	—

Five-Dollar Small-Size Silver Certificate, Special Yellow Seal, 1934A

Five-Dollar Small-Size Silver Certificate, Blue Seal, Series 1934B

10-Dollar Small-Size Silver Certificate, Blue Seal, Series 1933

10-Dollar Small-Size Silver Certificate, Special Yellow Seal, Series 1934A

	XF	CU		XF	CU
$10 1933	8,000.00	15,500.00	$10 1934B	400.00	1,400.00
$10 1933A	unique	—	$10 1934C	45.00	100.00
$10 1934	75.00	100.00	$10 1934D	50.00	125.00
$10 1934A	80.00	125.00	$10 1953	65.00	125.00
$10 1934, yellow seal	9,000.00	15,000.00	$10 1953A	125.00	200.00
$10 1934A, yellow seal	100.00	250.00	$10 1953B	75.00	150.00

FEDERAL RESERVE NOTES

The Federal Reserve System was created in 1913. Under this system there are 12 Federal Reserve Banks. They are governed in part by the U.S. government through the Federal Reserve Board, appointed by the president and confirmed by the Senate. Each of the Federal Reserve Banks is composed of various member banks. Today in the United States, the paper currency is not directly issued by the Treasury, but by the Federal Reserve Banks. Originally, Federal Reserve Notes bore an obligation of the government to redeem them in gold. This was changed in 1934. Today Federal Reserve Notes are the only type of paper money issued in the United States.

Just like all other currency, Federal Reserve Notes were reduced in size with the "series of 1928" in 1929.

Since 1993, major new innovations have been gradually incorporated into these notes to prevent counterfeiting. At first micro printing was incorporated into the design and around the frame of the portrait. Also, a transparent strip bearing the value and "USA" was imbedded inside the paper. It can only be seen when the note is held up to the light and cannot be photocopied.

These improvements were only a precursor to the first major overhaul of the designs of the currency since the 1920s. It incorporated these two, as well as other safeguards. Beginning in 1996 with the $100 note the portraits were enlarged to show more detail. The reverse was modified to incorporate more white space, making it possible to successfully use a watermark incorporated into the paper. This is an image neither printed on nor imbedded inside the paper, but one created by the pressure of a pattern pressed against the paper during its drying stage. Like the transparent printed strip, it can only be seen when the note is held up to the light. Among the most ingenious high-tech safeguards on the new notes is the use of color shifting ink, which alters its color depending on the angle of the light hitting it. The green Treasury seal has been retained, but the old letter seal indicating the Federal Reserve Bank of distribution is now replaced by the seal of the Federal Reserve system. These innovations were also incorporated into the 1996 series $50 and $20 notes, with the $10 and $5 notes following during the 1999 series. The $1 note is intended to remain basically the same.

Additional steps were taken to prevent counterfeiting in 2004. Both the $20 and $50 notes received multi-color background designs. The change also took place for the $10 and $100 notes in 2005.

A recent experiment with the use of a Web Press in the manufacture of $1 notes has resulted in less than total success. Interestingly enough for collectors, however, is the fact that this has resulted in some paper money being printed outside the Bureau of Engraving and Printing for the first time since the 19th century, and the appearance of an actual mintmark, FW used to designate Fort Worth, Texas.

Most Federal Reserve Notes since the 1930s are only collected in high grade. Dealers may be unwilling to buy even scarce pieces if not crisp uncirculated. Star replacement notes are quite popularly collected in this series, but again, must usually be crisp to be desirable. Very recent ones command no premium at all, and are sold at face value plus a handling fee to cover the dealer's labor.

★ ★ COUNTERFEIT ALERT ★ ★

Examine detail, silk threads in paper, and use reasonable caution. Circulating counterfeits exist, particularly $20, and to a lesser extent the $10. Most are imperfect, and can be easily detected on close examination. The $100 is the most counterfeited outside the United States.

10-Dollar Large-Size Federal Reserve Note, Red Seal, Series 1914

RED SEAL—SERIES OF 1914

	F	XF
$5 Abraham Lincoln/Columbus and Pilgrims	550.00	1,500.00
$10 Andrew Jackson/reaper and factory	675.00	1,500.00
$20 Grover Cleveland/train and ship	725.00	2,100.00
$50 Ulysses S. Grant/allegory of Panama	2,700.00	4,500.00
$100 Franklin/five allegories including commerce and agriculture	1,850.00	4,000.00

Five-Dollar Large-Size Federal Reserve Note, Blue Seal, Series 1914

10-Dollar Large-Size Federal Reserve Note, Blue Seal, Series 1914

1,000-Dollar Large-Size Federal Reserve Note, Blue Seal, Series 1918

BLUE SEAL—SERIES OF 1914

	F	XF
$5 Abraham Lincoln/Columbus and Pilgrims	100.00	200.00
$10 Andrew Jackson/Reaper and factory	110.00	240.00
$20 Grover Cleveland/train and ship	200.00	400.00
$50 Ulysses S. Grant/allegory of Panama	300.00	750.00
$100 Franklin/five allegories including commerce and agriculture	625.00	1,000.00

BLUE SEAL—SERIES OF 1918

	F	XF
$500 John Marshall/DeSoto discovering Mississippi	8,000.00	22,000.00
$1,000 Alexander Hamilton/eagle	9,200.00	24,000.00
$5,000 Madison *extremely rare*	—	
$10,000 Chase *extremely rare*	—	

SMALL SIZE NOTES—GREEN SEAL

$1 1963 Washington/great seal
$2 1976 Jefferson/Signing Declaration
$5 1928 Lincoln/Lincoln Memorial
$10 1928 Hamilton/Treasury Building
$20 1928 Jackson/White House
$50 1928 Grant/Capitol
$100 1928 Franklin/Independence Hall
$500 1928-34A McKinley/500
$1,000 1928-34A Cleveland/inscription
$5,000 1928-34B Madison/5,000
$10,000 1928-34B Chase/10,000

ONE DOLLAR

	F	XF
$1 1963	—	4.50
$1 1963A	—	3.50
$1 1963B	—	4.00
$1 1969	—	3.00
$1 1969A	—	3.00
$1 1969B	—	3.50
$1 1969C	—	3.50
$1 1969D	—	3.00

Five-Dollar Small-Size Federal Reserve Note, Green Seal, Series 1928A (obv.)

	F	XF
$1 1974	—	3.00
$1 1977	—	3.00
$1 1977A	—	3.00
$1 1981	—	3.00
$1 1981A	—	3.00
$1 1985	—	3.00
$1 1988	—	4.50
$1 1988A, DC	—	3.00
$1 1988A, FW	—	3.00
$1 1988A, web press	4.00	25.00
$1 1993, DC	—	3.00
$1 1993, FW	—	3.00
$1 1993, web press	3.00	12.00
$1 1995, DC	—	2.00
$1 1995, FW	—	2.00
$1 1995, web press	3.00	12.00
$1 1999, DC	—	2.00
$1 1999, FW	—	2.00
$1 2001, DC	—	2.00
$1 2001, FW	—	2.00
$1 2003, DC	—	2.00

	F	XF
$1 2003, FW	—	2.00
$1 2006, DC	—	2.00
$1 2006, FW	—	2.00

TWO DOLLARS

	XF	CU
$2 1976	—	5.00
$2 1995	—	15.00
$2 2003	—	4.00
$2 2003A	—	4.00

FIVE DOLLARS

	XF	CU
$5 1928	50.00	175.00
$5 1928A	60.00	150.00
$5 1928B	40.00	75.00
$5 1928C	220.00	600.00
$5 1928D	1,500.00	2,500.00

Five-Dollar Small-Size Federal Reserve Note, Green Seal, Series 1928A (rev.)

	XF	CU		XF	CU
$5 1934	25.00	55.00	$5 1950A	—	20.00
$5 1934A	18.00	40.00	$5 1950B	—	20.00
$5 1934, HAWAII	200.00	950.00	$5 1950C	—	17.00
$5 1934A, HAWAII	200.00	650.00	$5 1950D	—	25.00
$5 1934B	25.00	50.00	$5 1950E	—	55.00
$5 1934C	20.00	55.00	$5 1963	—	18.00
$5 1934D	25.00	60.00	$5 1963A	—	15.00
$5 1950	—	35.00			

Five-Dollar Small-Size Federal Reserve Note, Green Seal, Series 1969

	XF	CU
$5 1969	—	12.00
$5 1969A	—	13.00
$5 1969B	—	45.00
$5 1969C	—	12.00
$5 1974	—	10.00
$5 1977	—	10.00
$5 1977A	—	15.00
$5 1981	—	12.00
$5 1981A	—	15.00

	XF	CU
$5 1985	—	10.00
$5 1988	—	10.00
$5 1988A	—	10.00
$5 1993	—	10.00
$5 1995	—	9.00
$5 1999, large portrait	—	9.00
$5 2001	—	9.00
$5 2003, DC	—	10.00
$5 2003, FW	—	10.00
$5 2003A, FW	—	10.00
$5 2006, FW	—	9.00

10-Dollar Small-Size Federal Reserve Note, Green Seal, Series 1928

TEN DOLLARS

	XF	CU		XF	CU
$10 1928	100.00	180.00	$10 1934A	20.00	35.00
$10 1928A	80.00	200.00	$10 1934A, HAWAII	200.00	500.00
$10 1928B	40.00	75.00	$10 1934B	30.00	70.00
$10 1928C	150.00	450.00	$10 1934C	20.00	35.00
$10 1934	38.00	65.00	$10 1934D	25.00	55.00

10-Dollar Small-Size Federal Reserve Note, Green Seal, Series 1950A

	XF	CU		XF	CU
$10 1950	20.00	60.00	$10 1950D	—	30.00
$10 1950A	20.00	55.00	$10 1950E	—	95.00
$10 1950B	—	35.00	$10 1963	—	30.00
$10 1950C	—	40.00	$10 1963A	—	30.00

10-Dollar Small-Size Federal Reserve Note, Green Seal, Series 1969

	XF	CU		XF	CU
$10 1969	—	**25.00**	$10 1969C	—	**35.00**
$10 1969A	—	**20.00**	$10 1974	—	**25.00**
$10 1969B	—	**95.00**			

10-Dollar Small-Size Federal Reserve Note, Green Seal, Series 1977

10-Dollar Small-Size Federal Reserve Note, Green Seal, Series 2003

20-Dollar Small-Size Federal Reserve Note, Green Seal, Series 1928

TWENTY DOLLARS

	XF	CU
$10 1977	—	25.00
$10 1977A	—	25.00
$10 1981	—	30.00
$10 1981A	—	30.00
$10 1985	—	20.00
$10 1988A	—	20.00
$10 1990	—	20.00
$10 1993	—	15.00
$10 1995	—	15.00
$10 1999, large portrait	—	15.00
$10 2001	—	15.00
$10 2003, DC	—	15.00
$10 2003, FW	—	15.00
$10 2004A, FW	—	15.00
$10 2006, FW	—	15.00

	XF	CU
$20 1928	85.00	200.00
$20 1928A	150.00	400.00
$20 1928B	60.00	125.00
$20 1928C	850.00	2,500.00

20-Dollar Federal Reserve Note, Green Seal, Series 1934

20-Dollar Small-Size Federal Reserve Note, Green Seal, Series 1950D

20-Dollar Small-Size Federal Reserve Note, Green Seal, Series 2004

	XF	CU		XF	CU
$20 1934	40.00	75.00	$20 1977	—	45.00
$20 1934A	30.00	65.00	$20 1981	—	60.00
$20 1934, HAWAII	250.00	1,100.00	$20 1981A	—	45.00
$20 1934A, HAWAII	150.00	600.00	$20 1985	—	40.00
$20 1934B	40.00	90.00	$20 1988A	—	45.00
$20 1934C	40.00	65.00	$20 1990	—	35.00
$20 1934D	30.00	85.00	$20 1993	—	30.00
$20 1950	—	50.00	$20 1995	—	30.00
$20 1950A	—	50.00	$20 1996, large portrait	—	30.00
$20 1950B	—	45.00	$20 1999, large portrait	—	25.00
$20 1950C	—	50.00	$20 2001, DC, large portrait	—	25.00
$20 1950D	—	55.00			
$20 1950E	—	95.00	$20 2001, FW, large portrait	—	25.00
$20 1963	—	60.00			
$20 1963A	—	40.00	$20 2004, DC	—	25.00
$20 1969	—	45.00	$20 2004, FW	—	25.00
$20 1969A	—	55.00	$20 2004A, DC	—	25.00
$20 1969B	—	150.00	$20 2004A, FW	—	25.00
$20 1969C	—	45.00	$20 2006, DC	—	25.00
$20 1974	—	45.00	$20 2006, FW	—	25.00

50-Dollar Small-Size Federal Reserve Note, Green Seal, Series 1928

FIFTY DOLLARS

	XF	CU		XF	CU
$50 1928	375.00	550.00	$50 1934B	175.00	400.00
$50 1928A	110.00	375.00	$50 1934C	110.00	200.00
$50 1934	75.00	225.00	$50 1934D	150.00	250.00
$50 1934A	125.00	290.00			

50-Dollar Small-Size Federal Reserve Note, Green Seal, Series 1950

	XF	CU		XF	CU
$50 1950	95.00	175.00	$50 1950C	65.00	150.00
$50 1950A	90.00	180.00	$50 1950D	65.00	150.00
$50 1950B	70.00	125.00	$50 1950E	300.00	450.00

50-Dollar Small-Size Federal Reserve Note, Green Seal, Series 2004

	XF	CU
$50 1963A	—	100.00
$50 1969	—	125.00
$50 1969A	—	110.00
$50 1969B	—	900.00
$50 1969C	—	80.00
$50 1974	—	80.00
$50 1977	—	90.00
$50 1981	—	100.00
$50 1981A	—	120.00

	XF	CU
$50 1985	—	80.00
$50 1988	—	95.00
$50 1990	—	65.00
$50 1993	—	65.00
$50 1996, large portrait	—	60.00
$50 2001, large portrait	—	60.00
$50 2004, FW large portrait, colorized background	—	60.00
$50 2004A, FW	—	60.00
$50 2006, FW	—	60.00

100-Dollar Small-Size Federal Reserve Note, Green Seal, Series 1928A

ONE HUNDRED DOLLARS

	XF	CU
$100 1928	250.00	600.00
$100 1928A	250.00	300.00

100-Dollar Small-Size Federal Reserve Note, Green Seal, Series 1934B

	XF	CU		XF	CU
$100 1934	200.00	300.00	$100 1950A	—	200.00
$100 1934A	125.00	200.00	$100 1950B	—	200.00
$100 1934B	225.00	325.00	$100 1950C	—	175.00
$100 1934C	175.00	300.00	$100 1950D	—	200.00
$100 1934D	350.00	450.00	$100 1950E	—	400.00
$100 1950	—	350.00			

100-Dollar Small-Size Federal Reserve Note, Green Seal, Series 1996

	XF	CU
$100 1963A	—	175.00
$100 1969	—	160.00
$100 1969A	—	150.00
$100 1969C	—	150.00
$100 1974	—	140.00
$100 1977	—	140.00
$100 1981	—	175.00
$100 1981A	—	175.00
$100 1985	—	140.00
$100 1988	—	140.00

	XF	CU
$100 1990	—	135.00
$100 1993	—	135.00
$100 1996, large portrait	—	120.00
$100 1999, DC, large portrait	—	120.00
$100 1999, FW, large portrait	—	120.00
$100 2001, large portrait	—	120.00
$100 2003	—	120.00
$100 2003A	—	120.00
$100 2006, DC	—	120.00
$100 2006, FW	—	120.00

FIVE HUNDRED DOLLARS

	XF	CU
$500 1928	1,600.00	2,800.00
$500 1934	1,200.00	1,750.00
$500 1934A	1,000.00	1,600.00
$500 1934B	—	—
$500 1934C	—	—

ONE THOUSAND DOLLARS

	XF	CU
$1,000 1928	2,250.00	3,800.00
$1,000 1934	2,250.00	3,400.00
$1,000 1934A	2,000.00	3,200.00
$1,000 1934C	—	—

FIVE THOUSAND DOLLARS

	XF	CU
$5,000 1928	65,000.00	75,000.00
$5,000 1934	65,000.00	75,000.00
$5,000 1934A	—	—
$5,000 1934B	—	—

TEN THOUSAND DOLLARS

	XF	CU
$10,000 1928	75,000.00	150,000.00
$10,000 1934	60,000.00	80,000.00
$10,000 1934A	—	—
$10,000 1934B	—	—

FEDERAL RESERVE BANK NOTES

Federal Reserve Bank Notes are a type of national currency issued not by individual national banks but directly by the 12 federal reserve banks. These are regional banks under the partial control of the Board of Governors of the Federal Reserve, appointed by the president. Unlike Federal Reserve Notes, these were legal tender but not a government obligation. The obligation to redeem Federal Reserve Bank Notes fell with the individual Federal Reserve Banks and not directly with the Treasury. They were issued for a fairly short duration.

Small-size Federal Reserve Bank Notes are actually emergency currency printed on notes originally intended to become regular 1929 series national currency. The identity of the Federal Reserve Bank is printed where the name of the National Bank would have been, and small details of text are either blocked out or added. They were issued in 1933 and have a brown Treasury seal, unlike the large-size notes, which feature a blue one.

Star replacement notes are scarce and command a significant premium.

One-Dollar Large-Size Federal Reserve Bank Note, Series 1918

	F	XF
$1 1918 George Washington/eagle on flag	110.00	250.00
$2 1918 Thomas Jefferson/battleship	500.00	1,300.00
$5 1915 Abraham Lincoln/Columbus, Pilgrims landing	400.00	700.00
$5 1918 same	375.00	650.00
$10 1915 Andrew Jackson/horse-drawn reaper and factory	1,300.00	2,750.00
$10 1918 same	1,250.00	2,750.00
$20 1915 Grover Cleveland/train and ship	2,500.00	5,000.00
$20 1918 same	2,650.00	5,250.00
$50 1918 Ulysses S. Grant/allegory of Panama	9,500.00	17,000.00

Five-Dollar Small-Size Federal Reserve Bank Note, Brown Seal, Series 1929

SMALL-SIZE NOTES—BROWN SEAL

	F	XF		F	XF
$5 Boston	25.00	60.00	$10 Minneapolis	30.00	75.00
$5 New York	20.00	50.00	$10 Kansas City	25.00	50.00
$5 Philadelphia	20.00	75.00	$10 Dallas	300.00	800.00
$5 Cleveland	20.00	50.00	$10 San Francisco	200.00	500.00
$5 Atlanta	35.00	50.00	$20 Boston	30.00	75.00
$5 Chicago	20.00	50.00	$20 New York	35.00	50.00
$5 St. Louis	300.00	1,500.00	$20 Philadelphia	35.00	90.00
$5 Minneapolis	75.00	225.00	$20 Cleveland	30.00	70.00
$5 Kansas City	75.00	225.00	$20 Richmond	30.00	175.00
$5 Dallas	55.00	75.00	$20 Atlanta	35.00	150.00
$5 San Francisco	950.00	4,500.00	$20 Chicago	30.00	60.00
$10 Boston	30.00	75.00	$20 St. Louis	30.00	95.00
$10 New York	90.00	300.00	$20 Minneapolis	30.00	90.00
$10 Philadelphia	22.00	65.00	$20 Kansas City	35.00	150.00
$10 Cleveland	20.00	90.00	$20 Dallas	300.00	900.00
$10 Richmond	30.00	95.00	$20 San Francisco	100.00	200.00
$10 Atlanta	25.00	75.00	$50 New York	75.00	150.00
$10 Chicago	30.00	70.00	$50 Cleveland	70.00	115.00
$10 St. Louis	25.00	75.00	$50 Chicago	85.00	150.00

10-Dollar Small-Size Federal Reserve Bank Note, Brown Seal, Series 1929

20-Dollar Small-Size Federal Reserve Bank Note, Brown Seal, Series 1929

100-Dollar Small-Size Federal Reserve Bank Note, Brown Seal, Series 1929

	F	XF		F	XF
$50 Minneapolis	70.00	150.00	$100 Richmond	150.00	300.00
$50 Kansas City	75.00	160.00	$100 Chicago	150.00	225.00
$50 Dallas	375.00	1,700.00	$100 Minneapolis	150.00	250.00
$50 San Francisco	90.00	300.00	$100 Kansas City	125.00	210.00
$100 New York	130.00	175.00	$100 Dallas	400.00	1,500.00
$100 Cleveland	135.00	175.00			

CONFEDERATE STATES ISSUES

The story of Confederate paper money is in some ways reminiscent of that of Continental currency. Under desperate wartime circumstances, and with the best intentions, the government attempted to finance the war effort by printing unbacked paper currency. The initial series, backed by cotton, held its value at first and restraint was used in the quantities issued, but as the war continued more and more were printed, causing inflation. According to the legends on the later notes, they could not be redeemed until "two years after the ratification of a treaty of peace between the Confederate States and United States." Ultimately the seventh and final issue was authorized in unlimited quantity. After two billion dollars were issued, the currency's value eroded almost completely. Measured in gold dollars its decline can be seen as follows, along with rough quantities issued or authorized:

1861 March	$150,000,000	95¢
1862	$265,000,000	
1863	$515,000,000	33¢
1864	$1,000,000,000	
1865 April	none	1-2/3¢
1865 May	none	1/12¢

For many years Confederate currency was synonymous with worthlessness, and some people even burned it. From the 1960s onward it has taken on value as a collectible. Since the late 1990s, there has been a particularly strong market for this series. Prices have increased drastically.

The first issue of Confederate currency of March 1861 was initially issued in Montgomery, Ala., but the wording was changed to Richmond, Va. This is because the capitol of the Confederacy was moved to Richmond in May after Virginia withdrew from the Union. Throughout the war the production of Confederate notes was plagued with difficulties. The Northern printers, who had originally been hired to print notes before hostilities erupted, were no longer available. Paper was in short supply. It was also not always practical to import notes, paper or even plates due to the Union blockade of Southern ports. Some paper was brought in from the North by smugglers and from Great Britain by blockade runners. As a result some of the designs use improvised images not initially prepared for Confederate currency. More suitable images used include portraits of Confederate President Jefferson Davis and members of his cabinet, as well as of Southern agriculture.

★ ★ COUNTERFEIT ALERT ★ ★

It has been suggested that contemporary counterfeits were made of virtually every type of Confederate currency. True or false, it stands that a vast array of contemporary counterfeits of Confederate notes have survived. Most are printed from very crudely engraved plates. Like real examples, they are often printed on thin, limp paper. Not all the counterfeits made during the Civil War were actually meant to circulate. Samuel Upham of Philadelphia made 1-1/2 million Confederate and Southern state notes as a spoof, all with the notice "Facsimile Confederate Note—Sold wholesale and retail, by S.C. Upham, 403 Chestnut Street, Philadelphia" in the margin. Many had this notice cut off and intact examples are worth at least a few dollars each. In 1954 Cheerios cereal distributed reproductions as a promotion. Other similar notes printed on brittle brownish-yellow paper were printed in the 1960s. Many but not all have the word "FACSIMILE" near the margin.

Some "fantasy" notes were also made to circulate during the Civil War period. These were notes claiming to be Confederate, but with designs which the Confederate government never used. The most famous of these notes is the "female riding a deer" note, which actually depicted Artemis riding a stag. It is illustrated below. Most of the counterfeits, both contemporary and modern, have printed signatures, all authentic notes are hand signed except for the 50¢ denomination.

Reproduction
$100-Dollar Confederate Bill

FIRST ISSUE, MONTGOMERY 1861

	VG	VF
$50 Three slaves hoeing cotton	2,250.00	5,200.00
$100 Train.	850.00	4,400.00
$500 Train on bridge, cattle below	1,400.00	8,800.00
$1000 John Calhoun and Andrew Jackson	1,700.00	8,000.00

FIRST ISSUE, RICHMOND 1861

	VG	VF
$50 Industry and Agriculture seated on cotton	110.00	700.00
$100 Train.	140.00	750.00

SECOND ISSUE, JULY 25, 1861

	VG	VF
$5 Inscription	250.00	2,100.00
$5 Liberty and eagle, sailor left	220.00	1,600.00
$10 Liberty and eagle, Commerce left	38.00	450.00
$20 Sailing ship.	20.00	110.00
$20 Artemis riding stag, Indian seated left, Contemporary Fantasy	18.00	70.00
$50 Washington	22.00	125.00
$100 Ceres and Proserpina	110.00	700.00

THIRD ISSUE, SEPT. 2, 1861

	VG	VF
$2 Confederacy striking down Union, Judah Benjamin l.	90.00	400.00
$5 Cotton being loaded onto steamboat left, Indian princess right.	1,300.00	7,750.00
$5 Commerce seated on bale of cotton	17.00	45.00

Five-Dollar Commerce Seated on Bale, Third Issue

20-Dollar Industry Seated Behind Large 20, Third Issue

	VG	VF
$5 Allegories of Commerce, Agriculture, Liberty, Industry and Justice, Minerva left	80.00	500.00
$5 Sailor with cotton bales, C.G. Memminger left	32.00	75.00
$5 Boy's bust left, blacksmith seated right	130.00	700.00
$5 C.G. Memminger, V at lower right	27.00	85.00
same but contempory counterfiet	27.00	85.00
$5 same, but FIVE at lower right	27.00	85.00
$10 Liberty with eagle left	650.00	4,250.00
$10 Ceres and Commerce left	17.00	75.00
$10 Indian Family	80.00	425.00
$10 Cotton Picker	35.00	200.00
$10 Revolutionary War generals with sweet potatoes, Minerva standing r.	17.00	75.00

	VG	VF
$10 Wagon with cotton, John Ward left	200.00	950.00
$10 Robert Hunter left, child right	30.00	200.00
$10 Hope with anchor, Robert Hunter left, C.G. Memminger rt.	22.00	150.00
$10 same, with X X overprint	27.00	125.00
$20 Ceres between Commerce and Navigation	80.00	450.00
$20 Sailing ship	17.00	65.00
$20 Navigation seated with globe	350.00	1,800.00
$20 Industry seated behind large 20	12.00	50.00
$20 Alexander Stephens	40.00	200.00
$50 Moneta & chest	20.00	100.00
$50 Train	450.00	3,600.00
$50 Jefferson Davis	27.00	175.00
$100 Loading cotton onto wagon, sailor left	27.00	120.00

FOURTH ISSUE, APRIL 17, 1862

	VG	VF
$1 Steamship	22.00	100.00
$1 same with ONE overprint	26.00	140.00
$2 Confederacy striking down Union, Judah Benjamin l.	22.00	75.00
$2 same with "2 TWO" overprint	30.00	125.00
$10 Commerce reclining. *rare*	—	
$10 Ceres seated. *rare*	—	
$20 Liberty with shield	650.00	3,600.00
$100 Train	27.00	75.00
$100 Hoeing cotton	27.00	75.00

FIFTH ISSUE, DEC. 2, 1862

	VG	VF
$1 Clement Clay	26.00	85.00
$2 Judah Benjamin	24.00	75.00
$5 Confederate capitol at Richmond, Memminger right	12.00	42.00
$10 South Carolina capitol, Robert Hunter right	12.00	42.00
$20 Tennessee capitol, Alexander Stephens right	22.00	110.00
$50 Jefferson Davis	27.00	150.00
$100 Lucy Pickens	35.00	150.00

SIXTH ISSUE, APRIL 6, 1863

	VG	VF
50¢ Jefferson Davis	12.00	38.00
$1 Clement Clay	25.00	85.00
$2 Judah Benjamin	25.00	175.00
$5 Confederate capitol at Richmond, Memminger right	20.00	38.00
$10 South Carolina capitol, Robert Hunter right	18.00	45.00
$20 Tennessee capitol, Alexander Stephens right	16.00	50.00
$50 Jefferson Davis	22.00	75.00
$100 Lucy Pickens center, soldiers left, George Randolph right	27.00	85.00

50-Cent Jefferson Davis, Seventh Issue

10-Dollar Field Artillery, Robert Hunter Right, Seventh Issue

SEVENTH ISSUE, FEB. 17, 1864

	VG	VF
50¢ Jefferson Davis	10.00	35.00
$1 Clement Clay	32.00	110.00
$2 Judah Benjamin	27.00	85.00
$5 Confederate capitol at Richmond, Memminger right	10.00	35.00
$10 Field Artillery, Robert Hunter right	10.00	30.00
$20 Tennessee capitol, Alexander Stephens right	10.00	30.00
$50 Jefferson Davis	22.00	65.00
$100 Lucy Pickens, soldiers left, George Randolph right	27.00	70.00
$500 Flag and seal left, Stonewall Jackson right	130.00	450.00

Jefferson Davis 50-Dollar Confederate Note, Seventh Issue

Resources

CLUBS AND ASSOCIATIONS

Coin collecting can be an extremely social hobby, with national, regional and local clubs. The largest numismatic organization in the world is the American Numismatic Association. It is an institution chartered by Congress to promote numismatic knowledge, and has over the years attracted hundreds of thousands of collectors and dealers. Not only does it provide the arbitration services mentioned above, but holds large conventions twice each year at various locations throughout the country. The summer ANA convention is particularly important, as it is one of the largest coin shows in the world, including not only coin dealers but also representatives of the mints of many foreign countries. Other benefits to ANA membership include a circulating numismatic library, access to its one-week summer seminar in Colorado, and an authentication service. Every member of the ANA also receives a monthly issue of the *Numismatist*, its official journal containing many popular articles and columns, as well as ads by member dealers. Its address is:

> American Numismatic Association
> 818 North Cascade Ave.
> Colorado Springs, CO 80903
> www.money.org.

Another extremely important institution is the American Numismatic Society, which boasts the most important numismatic library in the Western Hemisphere. It has played a significant role in the promotion of original academic numismatic research, and there is little cutting edge scholarship in which its books or staff are not consulted. It also conducts a summer seminar for graduate students and scholarships for students incorporating numismatic research in their theses. Its address is:

> American Numismatic Society
> 96 Fulton Street
> New York, NY 10038 in the Financial District
> www.numismatics.org.

Many regional associations exist, and most of them sponsor important coin shows. One of the largest such organizations is F.U.N. or Florida United Numismatists, which sponsors a large show of national importance each January in Orlando. Another large regional organization is the Central States Numismatic Association which sponsors conventions throughout the Midwest. The addresses of some of the more important regional societies are:

Florida United Numismatists
POB 951988
Lake Mary, FL 32795

Central States Numismatic Society
POB 841
Logansport, IN 46947

Great Eastern Numismatic Association
1805 Weatherstone Drive
Paoli, PA 19301

New England Numismatic Association
POB 586
Needham, MA 02192

Pacific Northwest Numismatic Association
P.O. Box 4718
Federal Way, WA 98063-4718

There are, of course, a good many state level organizations, too numerous to mention here.

MUSEUMS

There is nothing for getting acquainted with numismatics like viewing the exhibits presented by a numismatic museum. It is an experience no beginner will soon forget. There are only two purely numismatic museums in the United States, but others also have respectable coin collections and numismatic exhibits. Both the American Numismatic Association in Colorado Springs and the American Numismatic Society in New York have very important museums with public exhibits of coins. The exhibits at either institution will give a good overview of the evolution of coinage and money over the last couple thousand years.

For decades the Smithsonian Institution in Washington, D.C. also has had a very significant numismatic collection on display, with notable pieces in the fields of United States and world gold, as well as of Russian coinage, among others. Recently it announced its intention to shut down its coin display in the near future. Some coins are featured on its Web site, www.si.edu.

Almost all museums have 99 percent of their holding stored in secure vaults, with selected representative coins on display. Museum curators are notably cooperative with scholars and serious collectors, however, and a call to the museum in advance can often arrange for the viewing of specimens not available to the general public.

Non-numismatic institutions with significant coin and/or paper money exhibits include the Federal Reserve Bank of New York (New York, N.Y.) and the Durham Western Heritage Museum (Omaha, Neb.).

Another way to see fairly interesting coins at a museum is to catch them in interdisciplinary exhibits. One good example was an exhibit of medieval armor mounted by the Metropolitan Museum of Art in New York. Accompanying the suits of armor were large medieval bracteate silver coins depicting similar armor in a contemporary manner. Other museums, including the Smithsonian, have followed this method of exhibiting too.

BOOKS ABOUT U.S. COINS

One cannot overemphasize the importance of books in fully understanding rare coins. The difference between a person accumulating a few interesting coins and a true numismatist is not how much a person spends, but how much a person learns.

The following books provide a good general background to U.S. coins. Those books dealing with particular coin series are sequenced in the same order in which series are sequenced in this book. (However, for the readers' benefit, other books are included about coins not covered in this book.) Don't be put off by early publication dates, as many standard works from earlier decades have been reprinted many times and are widely available through coin dealers. This is just a sampling; many other worthwhile books are available.

GENERAL U.S. COIN BOOKS

Berman, Allen G., *Warman's Coins and Paper Money*, 4th Ed. An expanded version of this book, also including ancients and world coins.

Bowers, Q. David, *The History of United States Coinage As Illustrated by the Garrett Collection.*

Breen, Walter, *Walter Breen's Complete Encyclopedia of U.S. and Colonial Coins.* One of the most intelligent in-depth general catalogs of the series. Excellent!

Breen, Walter, *Walter Breen's Encyclopedia of U.S. and Colonial Proof Coins.*

Fivaz, Bill and Stanton, J.T., *The Cherry Pickers' Guide to Rare Die Varieties.*

Yeoman, R.S., *A Guide Book of United States Coins.* Popularly called the "Red Book," it is the widely acknowledged Bible of U.S. coins.

Yeoman, R.S., *Handbook of United States Coins.* Popularly called the "Blue Book," a companion to the Red Book above, designed for those with an eye to selling their coins.

GRADING

American Numismatic Association, *Official A.N.A. Grading Standards for United States Coins.* No one has any business investing in U.S. coins, or even spending significant money on them as a hobby, if they don't have this book.

BOOKS ABOUT U.S. COINS

Professional Coin Grading Service, *Official Guide to Coin Grading and Counterfeit Detection.*

Ruddy, James F., *Photograde.*

DETECTING COUNTERFEITS

American Numismatic Association, *Counterfeit Detection*, two vols.

Fivaz, Bill, Bill Fivaz's *Counterfeit Detection Guide.* Convenient set of blow-up photos of authentic examples by a noted coin photographer.

Harshe, Bert, *How to Detect Altered & Counterfeit Coins and Paper Money.*

Kleeberg, John M., ed., *Circulating Counterfeits of the Americas*, American Numismatic Society, NY.

Larson, Charles M., *Numismatic Forgery.*

Lonesome, John, *Detecting Counterfeit Coins.*

Lonesome, John, *Detecting Counterfeit Gold Coins.*

Professional Coin Grading Service, *Official Guide to Coin Grading and Counterfeit Detection.*

Virtually every issue of *The Numismatist*, the official journal of the A.N.A., has large clear photographs of newly discovered counterfeits.

COLONIAL COINS

Breen, Walter, *Walter Breen's Complete Encyclopedia of U.S. and Colonial Coins.* Despite being a general book, it is also one of the best treatments of Colonials as well.

Crosby, S.S., *The Early Coins of America.*

Kleeberg, John, *Money of Pre-Federal America.*

Maris, Edward, *A Historical Sketch of the Coins of New Jersey.*

Miller, Henry Clay, *State Coinages of Connecticut.*

Newman, Eric P., ed., *Studies on Money in Early America.*

Noe, Sydney, *The New England and Willow Tree Coinage of Massachusetts.*

Noe, Sydney, *The Oak Tree Coinage of Massachusetts.*

Noe, Sydney, *The Pine Tree Coinage of Massachusetts.*

Richardson, A.D., *The Copper Coins of Vermont.* (An extension of the standard numbering system established in Ryder, Hillyer, *The Colonial Coins of Vermont*).

Vlack, Robert, *Early American Coins.*

HALF CENTS
Breen, W., *Walter Breen's Encyclopedia of United States Half Cents 1793-1857.*

Cohen, Roger, *American Half Cents, The "Little Half Sisters."* Establishes a standard numbering system for die varieties.

LARGE CENTS
Newcomb, H., *United States Copper Cents 1816-1857.* (Covers die varieties).

Sheldon, William, *Penny Whimsy*, 1958. (Covers die varieties 1793 to 1815, a standard which has lived through many reprints).

SMALL CENTS
Snow, *Flying Eagle and Indian Cents.*

Taylor, *The Standard Guide to the Lincoln Cent.*

Wiles, James, *The RPM Book—Lincoln Cents.* Guide to repunched mintmark varieties.

TWO-CENT AND THREE-CENT PIECES
Bowers, Q. David, *U.S. Three-Cent and Five-Cent Pieces.*

Flynn, Kevin, *Getting Your Two Cents Worth.*

Kilman, M., *The Two Cent Piece and Varieties, 1977.*

HALF DIMES AND NICKELS
Blythe, Al, *The Complete Guide to Liberty Seated Half Dimes.*

Bowers, Q. David, *U.S. Three-Cent and Five-Cent Pieces.*

Lange, David, *The Complete Guide to Buffalo Nickels.*

Valentine, D.W., *The United States Half Dimes,* 1931. Standard reference on die varieties for the series.

Wescott, Michael, *The United States Nickel Five-Cent Piece.*

DIMES

Bowers, Q. David, *United States Dimes, Quarters, and Half Dollars.*

Greer, Brian, *The Complete Guide to Liberty Seated Dimes.*

Lange, David W., *The Complete Guide to Mercury Dimes.*

Lawrence, David, *The Complete Guide to Barber Dimes.*

Rapsus, Ginger, *The United States Clad Coinage.*

TWENTY-CENT PIECES AND QUARTERS

Bowers, Q. David, *United States Dimes, Quarters, and Half Dollars.*

Briggs, Larry, *Liberty Seated Quarters.*

Browning, A. W., *The Early Quarter Dollars of the United States.* Standard reference on die varieties for the series.

Cline, J.H., *Standing Liberty Quarters*

Hammer, Ted, "The Twenty Cent Piece," *The Numismatist*, vol. 60, pp. 167-69.

Lawrence, David, *The Complete Guide to Barber Quarters.*

Rapsus, Ginger, *The United States Clad Coinage.*

HALF DOLLARS

Bowers, Q. David, *United States Dimes, Quarters and Half Dollars.*

Fox, Bruce, *The Complete Guide to Walking Liberty Half Dollars.*

Lawrence, David, *The Complete Guide to Barber Halves.*

Overton, Al C., *Early Half Dollar Die Varieties 1794-1836.* Standard reference on die varieties for the series.

Rapsus, Ginger, *The United States Clad Coinage.*

SILVER & CLAD DOLLARS

Bolender, M.H., *The United States Early Silver Dollars from 1794 to 1803.* Standard reference on die varieties for the series.

Bowers, Q. David, *Silver Dollars and Trade Dollars of the United States: A Complete Encyclopedia.*

Newman, Eric, and Bressett, Kenneth, *The Fantastic 1804 Dollar.*

Rapsus, Ginger, *The United States Clad Coinage.*

Van Allen, Leroy, and Mallis, A. George, *Comprehensive Catalogue and Encyclopedia of U.S. Morgan and Peace Silver Dollars.*

Willem, John M., *The United States Trade Dollar.*

GOLD COINAGE

Akers, David, *Handbook of 20th-Century United States Gold Coins.*

Bowers, Q. David, *United States Gold Coins: An Illustrated History.*

COMMEMORATIVES

Bowers, Q. David, *Commemorative Coins of the United States: A Complete Encyclopedia.*

Hodder, Michael and Bowers, Q. David, *A Basic Guide to United States Commemorative Coins.*

Swiatek, Anthony and Breen, Walter, *Encyclopedia of United States Silver and Gold Commemorative Coins 1892-1989.*

PROOFS

Breen, Walter, *Walter Breen's Encyclopedia of United States and Colonial Proof Coins.*

PATTERNS

Judd, J. Hewett, *United States Pattern, Experimental and Trial Pieces.* The newest edition of this standard has been updated by Q. David Bowers.

Krause, Chester, and Mishler, Clifford, *Standard Catalog of World Coins* and *Standard Catalog of World Coins, 19th Century.*

ERRORS

Margolis, Arnold, *Error Coin Encyclopedia.*

Spadone, Frank, *Major Variety and Oddity.*

Wiles, James, and Miller, Tom, *The RPM Book.* Guide to repunched mintmark varieties.

TOKENS

Alpert, Stephen and Smith, Kenneth E., *Video Arcade, Pinball, Slot Machine, and other Amusement Tokens of North America.*

Breen, Walter, *Pioneer and Fractional Gold.*

Coffee, John, and Ford, Harold, *Atwood-Coffee Catalogue of United States and Canadian Transportation Tokens*, 5th ed.

Fuld, George and Melvin, *Patriotic Civil War Tokens.*

Fuld, George and Melvin, *U. S. Civil War Store Cards.*

Hibler, Harold and Kappen, Charles, *So-Called Dollars.* A standard work on dollar sized tokens or medals, particularly those used temporarily as a medium of exchange or to represent such satirically.

Hodder, Michael J. and Bowers, Q. David, *Standard Catalogue of Encased Postage Stamps.*

Kagin, Donald, *Private Gold Coins and Patterns of the United States.*

Rulau, Russell, *Standard Catalog of United States Tokens.*

Rulau R. and Fuld,G., *Medallic Portraits of Washington.*

Schenkman, David, *Civil War Suttler Tokens and Cardboard Scrip.*

Sullivan, Edmund B., *American Political Badges and Medalets 1789-1892.*

Token and Medal Society, *TAMS Journal.* The journal of this organization is incredibly useful, with regular listing identifying "mavericks," or private tokens which bear no specific indication of their origin.

HAWAII, ALASKA, U.S. PHILIPPINES

Basso, Aldo, *Coins, Medals and Tokens of the Philippines.*

Gould, Maurice, *Hawaiian Coins, Tokens and Paper Money.*

Krause & Mishler, *Standard Catalog of World Coins*

Yeoman, R.S., *Guidebook of United States Coins*

CONFEDERATE COINS

Reed, Fred L., III, series of articles, *Coin World*, Oct. 4, Oct. 11, Oct. 18, 1989

PERIODICALS ABOUT U.S. COINS

Magazines have a certain immediacy not possible in books. They also put the reader in touch with the opinions of fellow numismatists.

CoinAge (monthly)—A popular newsstand magazine, oriented to the collector and the layman.

Coin Prices (six per year)—Extensive listings of United States coin values in many grades. Articles more oriented towards the market than towards history. Published by Krause Publications, the world's largest numismatic publisher.

Coins (monthly)—Very similar to *CoinAge* but put out by Krause Publications, the world's largest numismatic publisher.

CoinValues (monthly)—Extensive listings of United States coin values in many grades. Published by *Coin World*.

Coin World (weekly)—The largest circulation coin newspaper, covering both American and world coins.

Counterfeit Coin Bulletin (three times per year)—Detailed reports on newly discovered counterfeits. A joint publication of the American Numismatic Association and the International Association of Professional Numismatists.

Numismatic News (weekly)—A Krause Publications newspaper focusing primarily on United States coins.

The Numismatist (monthly)—The monthly journal of the American Numismatic Association. All full members receive a subscription.

BOOKS ABOUT U.S. PAPER MONEY

Berman, Allen G., *Warman's Coins & Paper Money, Identification and Price Guide*, 4th ed.

Cuhaj, George S., ed. *Standard Catalog of United States Paper Money*, 27th ed.

Lindquist, Scott & Schwartz, John, *Standard Guide to Small Size U.S. Paper Money: 1928 to Date*, 8th ed.

Lee, Wallace G., *Michigan 19th Century Obsolete Bank & Scrip Notes/ National Bank Notes 1863-1935*.

Newman, Eric P., *The Early Paper Money of America: Colonial Currency 1696-1810*, 5th ed.

Index